WHY NOT YOU

WHY NOT YOU

A LEADERSHIP GUIDE FOR THE CHANGE-MAKERS OF TOMORROW

CHRISTINA HALE

LIONCREST
PUBLISHING

WHY NOT YOU
A Leadership Guide for the Change-Makers of Tomorrow

ISBN   978-1-5445-3056-7   *Hardcover*
       978-1-5445-3055-0   *Paperback*
       978-1-5445-3054-3   *Ebook*

To my Gunga and Grandma Pedro, little girls who grew from unfathomable loss and loved so well. You are both long gone, yet you still help me every day. Thank you, thank you.

This book references youth, alcohol abuse, and sexual assault. If this is difficult for you, or if you just feel like you need to speak to someone, please call 1-800-656-HOPE, the free and confidential national sexual assault hotline, for support, advice, information, or a referral. It doesn't matter where you live in the United States, they will take your call 24/7 and, if need be, refer you to a service closer to home.

CONTENTS

THIS BOOK IS *NOT* ABOUT POLITICS, IT'S ABOUT POSITIONAL LEADERSHIP

First things first: I want you to know that I really don't care what your politics are. It's not my concern whether we disagree about this or that issue. In fact, I *hope* we disagree: it means you are thinking for yourself, which is one of the most important attributes of a **positional leader**. (Positional leadership is something you'll hear a *lot* more about over the course of this book.)

Through the following chapters, inevitably you'll get a strong inkling as to where I stand on a number of issues, and of course, there's nothing stopping you from finding out more (all it takes is a quick Google search or following me on social media). But I can't stress this enough: **I don't care what your politics are.** What matters to me is that you are in this for the right reasons, that you are following your *own* values.

What matters is that you lead not just with integrity but also a burning desire to *get things done*. Above all, that means being open to compromise. Remember, what starts as just an idea—something you feel passionate about and becomes a powerful talking point for you—could one day become your own piece of legislation. But in order for that to happen, to get your idea all the way across the finish line, you'll absolutely need to listen to and engage with diverging opinions.

Everyone's heard the expression *don't let the perfect become the enemy of the good*. But in practice, it can be hard to let go of the "perfect" version of your idea. I am here to tell you: if you want to get over the hump so that your idea can become the solution-based policy you've long dreamed of, you **can't have an all-or-nothing mentality.** You have to be willing to alter your idea and let others influence its outcome. You have to be okay with the outcome being a little different, even a little *less*, than you wanted.

Say you're pushing for a clean water act. Even if what emerges isn't as well-funded as you wished, or doesn't match how you originally conceived the bill, you'll have still succeeded in ensuring that kids in troubled areas have access to clean water. That's what counts, that *they* will be safer because of your idea and your effort. Is it perfect? No. Is there more work to be done? Absolutely. But in almost every case, helping move the needle forward is vastly better than not helping at all.

And that's what positional leadership is all about. It's what being a true changemaker is about: *getting up, getting it done, and then getting up to do it again. You've got work to do!*

I don't have to tell you how high the stakes are or how much work there is to do out there in our neighborhoods and communities to help make a better world. But none of it is possible if you just let your good ideas sit on the shelf in the library of your mind. In order to get them out of your head and into law, you have to **be resilient and keep pushing.**

FOREWORD

by MIKE SCHMUHL

Someone once told me that there are two lines of work where a young person is given a lot more responsibility than normal: public service and the military. In these jobs, young people are often the driving force behind the safety, security, freedoms, and policy implications for millions of people. More than twenty years into this century, and with so much disruption around the world on so many fronts, I would change that adage and say that young people can become involved in nearly *any* industry or field and make immediate and significant change.

In *Why Not You?*, my friend Christina Hale shares her own story along with some universal and helpful principles for a young person to find their calling and how they can follow their own path to make a difference and serve with focus, passion, and humility. Christina's life and outlook is inspiring, and she is the perfect storyteller to write this guide. She has experience in servant leadership roles and leading campaigns at local, state, federal, and international levels. While only each person can decide what they want to do or what they want to change, this book helps each person think about how to make it happen.

When I look back on my career in politics and public service, I'm amazed at how the simple decision to get involved in my local community and create change made everything else possible. I moved back home to Indiana in 2009 to work for my local congressman, Joe Donnelly. He asked me to manage his tough reelection effort (we won), and that first lap created opportunities for me to manage a mayoral race, become a city chief of staff, become a political strategist, lead a presidential campaign, and assume the role of party chair for our home state.

I think leading the Pete for America campaign is a good example as you begin to read Christina's book. Back in the early days of the presidential exploratory effort in 2019, national journalists and big contenders weren't asking Pete Buttigieg, *Why Not You?* They were wondering, *Who?*

Our small office had donated furniture and Wi-Fi hotspots. Three college interns about equaled the number of unpaid staff members on the team. We were up against some huge names in American politics. What did we have?

It turns out, we had a lot going for us. We had fresh ideas and a clear message and messenger. We tried to be more innovative and create a culture of belonging at a time when so many people were (and still are) turned off by politics. At the end of the cycle, our campaign became the largest in the history of Indiana and now-Secretary Buttigieg became the first LGBTQ+ presidential candidate in American history to be awarded national party delegates.

Through the ups and downs of politics over the years, one constant remains: I am proudest when I think about the young people I have worked alongside on efforts great and small. So many have gone on to do remarkable things, build impressive careers, and become positive forces in their fields and in their communities. While everyone comes from a different background or lived experience, they all stepped up with a common purpose: to serve others and make a positive change in the world. You can do it too, and it's never too late to take that first step.

Do you remember those days when you still thought life was all about smiles and picnics? Waking up to the things that need to change is never easy. As hard as it can be, you'll be glad you did.

HEEDING THE CALL

Sometimes you already *know* what motivates you. For whatever reason, it just resonates with you. You feel it in your heart.

But other times, the spark that sets in motion your journey as a changemaker comes from a place outside your control—and often, it is a dark place. The very thing that ultimately fuels your strength and conviction is what now haunts you, keeping you up at night, making your mind race.

I know because I was the same way.

It's something you can't plan for: that crazy, scary rush of adrenaline that makes you feel more sickeningly wide awake than you ever thought possible. Time slows down, your head throbs, and your heart races. It feels *all kinds of wrong*, and you can't help but think, *Hey! I'm just a kid. This isn't fair! This shouldn't be happening! I shouldn't be here! I don't know how to make this stop. I just want to put it back the way it was...*

Well, it may not be fair. But whatever happened, the hard truth is that the genie cannot be put back in the bottle. Things will never be the same.

Maybe you feel like you've lost a piece of yourself. But what you will ultimately discover is that what seemed like a curse can actually be a blessing in disguise, in that it leads to a heightened sense of right and wrong—and perhaps even a calling, deep within you, to be part of something bigger.

What sets your hair on fire?

It was the summer between eighth and ninth grade that I got the knock on my window in the middle of the night. I was only thirteen. But my birthday was coming up. I couldn't wait to be fourteen.

Actually, this was the second time that summer that someone had knocked at my window. A few weeks earlier, my friends had been drinking alcohol down at the beach—this was back in Long Beach, Indiana, the little lake town where I grew up. A few of them had gotten into real trouble, too drunk to walk home. So, they came and tapped at my window in the middle of the night. At first, I was petrified. My older brother had always done a masterly job of filling my head with ghost stories and such. And even though I was only thirteen, I had seen my share of horror movies and knew that the psycho killer always came after teenagers!

Thankfully, it wasn't a slasher. I heard my friends' voices: "Christie! Wake up!" In my neighborhood, kids looked out for one another. I opened my window and listened as they explained the situation. Finally, I agreed to head out with them and help carry the drunken ones home.

Now, weeks later, there was the *tap-tap-tap* again. "Christie! Christie!"

But this time, it was a different kind of crisis entirely.

The fact that I had been reading a Stephen King novel—alone in bed late at night!—didn't help matters. There was the adrenaline again: it flooded my body and brain all at once. *What was it this time? Were my friends in trouble again?* They certainly hadn't seemed inclined to repeat the disaster from earlier that summer, especially after their hangovers and the fury of their parents.

Yet, as it turns out, it was the worst kind of trouble. Much worse than what had happened before. **It would take me years to understand just how profound an impact that tap at my window would have on my life. It was one of those moments that doesn't come with an instruction manual.**

Turned out that the tapping on my window wasn't the same group as before. It was my friend Gabby (not her real name, but she could have been anybody). Her big sister had taken her to a total smash party like you only see in movies, full of older teens, kids who tested and broke limits. And yes, there was a lot of alcohol.

We had all been jealous of Gabby. She seemed so lucky to have a sister who let her tag along. The way we saw it, Gabby had won the social lottery.

It's crazy to think that back then I saw her as the lucky one: my cool friend with the big sister who would take her along to the high-school parties before she belonged there herself. If anything, I remember worrying that she wouldn't have time to be friends with me anymore. So, when she knocked on my window, shattered with tears and emotion, of course I opened and let her in.

Eventually, she was able to tell me her story, but at first, it came out in bits and pieces. She talked about the thrill of drinking her first keg cup of beer, handed to her by a nice girl who had made her laugh. Then, she described what the house was like and who else was there. But apparently, she didn't remember a whole lot after that.

Her next memory, she finally revealed to me, was of waking up in agony. Someone who she had known and liked, a popular guy (actually, it was her sister's best friend's boyfriend), was forcibly penetrating her. He was on top of her, holding her down.

It was even worse than that. In the dim light, I could see the swelling and cuts on Gabby's face. She had trouble getting all the words out. But the gist was clear: the experience had been excruciating, terrifying, and painful, and the perpetrator had left her with no escape. Then, when the nightmare had finally ended and her rapist was gone, that was when the shame and fear kicked in.

To this day, I think of how strong Gabby must have been to leave that room, find her sister, and get the hell out of there.

But in the moment, I didn't know what to do or who to tell. (Really could have used that instruction manual!) Gabby had come to me for help. But back then I wasn't ready. As we sat together, I realized her biggest concern was protecting her sister. That's probably the real reason she came to me that night. She was afraid of all the wrong things, and honestly, so was I. Would the truth put her sister in a bad position? Would she get kids at the party in trouble for drinking? She didn't want to get in trouble herself either—she wasn't sure if she had done something bad or if something bad had happened to her.

I was confused as well. No one had prepared us for this kind of violence. My friends and I had grown up in a world that felt very safe. In our small town, everybody knew everybody. Nobody really got in any kind of *big* trouble.

I kind of knew what rape was, but never expected something like this to happen to me or one of my friends. Gabby was in trouble and needed help—but, at the time, I mistakenly thought it was something we had to keep secret. Somehow, I had internalized that being a victim of assault is just not something you talked about, or even admitted to. We were so concerned (wrongly!) about protecting our reputations among our friends and not getting in trouble with our parents. Again, rape and sexual assault weren't a societal problem that we had heard much about or identified with in any way. But we would later learn how very common it is.

In the end, Gabby needed a doctor. She needed a parent. She needed real help, and all she had was me, a thirteen-year-old kid, full of empathy and bad advice. **I just knew that something was terribly, terribly wrong—but it was hard to understand what it was or what to do about it.**

Thirteen-year-old me wasn't educated or empowered enough to do much to help, but I was determined to change that and pay it forward one day. Much later, when I was elected and became a lawmaker myself, that is exactly what I did. And while I will always deeply regret not being there for Gabby in the way I wish I had, I did find a way ultimately to make positive change that would protect others from sexual assault.

And that is what this book is about: taking everything in your heart, the ideals as well as the scars, and making something *good* from them all.

Keeping your own mistakes and heartaches in mind, ask yourself these questions: *Do you have a good heart? Do you have a good mind? Are you in it for the right reasons? Are you satisfied with the status quo, or are you compelled to do all you can to bring about positive change in people's lives and help eliminate unnecessary pain and suffering?*

You know the answers. Now it's time to get ready.

A MOMENT OF AWAKENING

When I think of Gabby and what happened that summer, I realize nothing was ever the same after the violent crime committed against my friend. Before that point, I had a certain view about the world. By the end of the summer, and after I had started high school, it was like the brutal realities of the world had suddenly come crashing into my consciousness.

Yet, I am grateful for how my eyes were opened. It was through the experience of my friend that I was awakened to the issue of sexual assault—and came to realize the extent to which girls, and boys, can be vulnerable to this kind of behavior. I didn't know it then, but protecting people, especially young people, from sexual violence and harassment would one day become my primary focus and biggest issue as an elected lawmaker.

That happened many years later, of course. There were a lot of interim steps along my path, a lot of dots that still needed to be connected—between the thirteen-year-old girl I was and the empowered advocate I would become. But through it all, there was a common denominator: a passion for service, particularly for preventing sexual assault and supporting survivors.

It all started with that knock on the window. That was my moment.

You will have a moment like this too. You'll know when it happens. It's **the moment when your consciousness is awakened, and you become a different person** than before. Whether or not you have experienced it yet, you have likely heard the ringing, however distant, of this call to service. It's why you picked up this book, because you want to be a leader and change-maker for the issue or issues you care about. Maybe you're not quite there: you're still holding yourself back, not showing that side of yourself in certain social situations. Maybe you don't know where to channel your energy. Or you're skeptical about how much of a difference you can really make anyway.

Truth is, you *do* have a tough road ahead. The so-called "adults in the room," the ones making the decisions that affect us all, are not going to save you. *You* are the one who is going to have to make the trains run on time.

If you want to change the world, you're going to have to accept that *you're* the adult in the room—and that means stepping into your full potential as a leader and decision-maker.

It means embracing positional power.

POSITIONAL POWER

As much as the adults in charge can let us down, it's not a justification for apathy. And it certainly doesn't mean you're going to be able to drive meaningful change if you're ducking life in your parents' basement playing video games. You have to get out in the world and **seek top leadership roles where you can actually make decisions that drive policy.**

Positional leadership means you're the decision-maker; you're proposing legislation; you're the CEO of the organization that tackles the issues. In other words, you're not just helping bring the solutions; you're driving the whole ship.

But it's never about the title or the prestige. It's about being positioned to make positive change and help others who are still on the sidelines.

If you just want the big, fancy title, then put this book down right now and give it to someone who actually cares. But if you have a genuine servant-leader's mindset and are eager to prepare for positional leadership, then this book is for you.

It may sound weird to think of yourself this way, as a change-maker of tomorrow; you may not be fully comfortable with the role yet. If you're like many young people I talk to, you're still struggling with trying to find your place in the world. I understand: it's hard to stick your neck out, to go against the grain and speak your truth, especially when you're young. That said, it's important to recognize that even finding your courage to speak truth to power is not enough. It is also critically important to be empowered *yourself*. The good news: now you are on your way.

Regardless of where you are on your journey, you've found this book because you're on fire to make the world better—to set up others for success. For that, instead of applauding, I'm going to encourage you to dream even bigger. Rather than being satisfied with showing up when asked and talking about the change you'd like to see, you're going to have to take a step further and become a powerful advocate for the causes that inspire you and the communities you care so deeply about.

After all, **why *not* you?**

No one else is going to do it for you. But the more you put yourself out there, speak out for what you believe in, and embrace positional leadership, the more natural it will feel—and the more you'll be inspired to take up the calling to serve.

I know because I've seen it.

WHO AM I?

Some people, including my own brothers, would say that I am just a loser. More on that shortly. For now, let me introduce myself by saying I am the first Latina to serve in my community as an elected member of the Indiana General Assembly and to run for statewide office in Indiana. In 2020, I was also a nominee in my state for US Congress, in a race that was heralded as one of the most competitive in the country. *BeLatina* magazine described me as a "doer with the right intentions and the right goals to benefit all, not just the few at the top," and I have I worked hard at a career of paying it forward for the people and causes I care about so much.

But it wasn't always that way. High school wasn't an easy time for me. It was a journey of little heartbreaks; the ground never seemed very solid underfoot, and to be honest, my friends didn't feel very solid either. It was a lonely time, and trouble was always around. Finally, the day came when I had to have a difficult conversation with my family. I was pregnant, unprepared, and scared to death. It was the day my brothers called me a loser. It was also the day that eventually gave me the insight and strength to take the crucial step from caring about issues to being a change-maker myself.

Our disappointments, challenges, mistakes, and tragedies—as well as triumphs—are what make us uniquely ourselves.

Through the course of this book, you're going to gain a new confidence that comes from hearing about others like you who did (and do) amazing things and leave their impressive footsteps to follow. In my career—both as a lawmaker and working with youth and adult leaders all over the world—I have witnessed some of the most extraordinary change-makers out there today. Some of them are people you've heard about. Others are unsung heroes.

But this is a book about *you* and how you can become one of the positional leaders of tomorrow we so desperately need. Again, it's *not* a book about politics. You and I may not agree on issues, philosophies, or political parties. So what? Who cares? We *can* agree, I'm sure, that there are huge problems needing to be fixed and challenges to be addressed. I am also certain we can agree that we need more sincerely motivated people prepared to step up and become part of the process, rather than just get into fights on social media. Different people will have different solutions. I'm not here to tell you what the right or wrong solutions are. Rather, my goal is to inspire and empower readers from all walks of life—who each have their distinct sets of experiences and values—to embrace an ambitious agenda and a positional leadership that is authentic to them.

As individuals who want to drive positive change, you'll be drawn instinctively to the issue or issues that speak to *you*, that motivate you to jump from the sidelines and become an actor in the game of life. As with my moment of awakening, you'll become passionate about your cause, maybe more passionate than anyone else, because it's an issue that's either touched you personally or impacted someone you love. Maybe most importantly, it's an issue that will affect those who come *after* you—it's up to you to make the change now, so they don't suffer the consequences.

In my case, my calling to serve began as a single moment, but then sadly, I saw how sexual assault was something that happened to a number of my friends in high school and in college. I realized that this was impacting girls, and boys too, all over the world, from Yemen to Niger to California. **It is something that has to stop.**

For me, what began as a single moment—when my heart and mind were opened, personally, to a broad societal problem—evolved into something that went way beyond just my circle. I learned that this issue was personal to many other people. Because of my connection and my experiences, I had the will and motivation to drive change, for all of them and all of us.

WHO ARE YOU?

This is not a book about sexual assault. But it is a book about the causes that need our attention and how you really don't have a choice. You need to get yourself prepared in your heart and your mind because only you can make these changes. I'm not being dramatic. It may well come down to you and only you. Whether gun violence in your school or clean water in your community, the issues that matter most to you can only truly be understood by you. No one else possesses your unique set of experiences and perspectives.

The problem is that sometimes we think we're not good enough, not worthy, or not prepared enough to do something about the problem. We might care strongly about the issue, but our own self-talk bogs us down: *How can I possibly, as an army of one, do something that could make things better for everyone? Who am I to jump into this?*

Does this sound familiar? Maybe you're worried that you're not smart enough, not a good speaker, not charismatic. I'm going to be very real here and tell you something that you probably don't want to hear: whatever it is that you fear or second-guess about yourself—that you're not good-looking enough, not athletic enough—you're probably right about it. And that's okay. Let me explain.

I speak from experience: as a little kid growing up in mostly white Indiana, I really, really hated my arms. They didn't look like other kids' arms, even those of the boys. No, mine were even hairier, like my mom's and my grandma's. I didn't wear short sleeves because I was so embarrassed by them. In fact, one time I got busted by my best friend—at a Brownie meeting of all places—for having shaved them. I remember it like yesterday. It was my first troop meeting and first chance to wear my brand-new uniform. My mom had sewed on my merit patches, and I was beyond excited. So, that morning, I secretly borrowed my dad's electric razor and shaved the dark hair from my arms. Walking into that group of girls, I felt like Wonder Woman the first time she caught sight of herself in her red boots and bullet-repelling bracelets. But then my friend called me out. And she wasn't quiet about it, either. Pretty soon the room full of Brownies was examining my arms, the crowd pushing little-girl me to confess to my crime. Deeply embarrassed at being busted, I ran all the way back home. I couldn't show my hairy arms after that. In fact, from that day until I graduated from high school, I did my best to never be seen in short sleeves. We all suffer from our own kind of brainwashing about our perceived shortcomings.

Knowing that I am now a positional leader fighting for systemic change to help people be successful, I accept my arms for the gift they are. This is very important for me. When I see my arms, I see all the kids who didn't fit in with their communities.

Things that happen in life when we are little may seem silly when we grow older, but they're not. They are formative. I ask you to think about those little humiliations and traumas you lived through as a much younger kid. Take some time to remember.

Today, if I happen to be interviewing with the *New York Times* or giving a high-profile TED Talk, you can bet that I am very aware of my hairy arms. My arms remind me of the traumatic childhood experience and why I need to seize the strength to push back for the little kids like me (who should never be ashamed for coming from somewhere else or looking different). My arms won't let me forget who and what is most important and what my role needs to be for them. I can't be there for every lone person, depressed or bullied, but I can scale up my impact to help.

So, if you're worried that you don't compare well to so-and-so in this or that respect, I don't mean to be harsh... but you're probably right. There's always going to be someone who's cleverer, who has better clothes, or whatever the case may be. So what? Who cares? Are you going to go through your whole life worrying about things like that? In the grand scheme, they really don't matter, and in fact, **these "imperfections" are going to make you even more powerful**—because they are your pathway to greater empathy and understanding.

There is no such thing as a
perfect person, but there are good
people who do good for others.

There is nobility in our imperfection. It's what makes us uniquely ourselves; it's what gives us our stories. Think back to all those daggers to your heart, all the times you've been betrayed by a friend, or had your feelings hurt, or been disappointed by someone, even by those who are supposed to be your greatest supporters. Those sharp little knives hurt, no getting around it. But you know what? You're probably going to be hurt in life again.

By focusing on something bigger than yourself, by making positive change for others, little by little you start to get over the hurt. You develop character and become a richer human being, a stronger, more effective change-maker for your cause. Not only that, but you're able to help others navigate around *their* worries and imperfections.

The title of this book is *Why Not You?* Well, I'm here to tell you that the answer is you. **You're exactly the right person for this job.** The power of your story gives you credibility and resilience to make things better for everyone else, to fight for clean water, freedom from violence, and so much more. And if *you* don't step up—don't use the power of your story to do good—you might never forgive yourself.

So, come forth and bring your full, authentic self to the table—your experience, your passion, your insight into what are all the small fixes that are going to contribute to systemic change. Authenticity is key. You care deeply not just because you read about something in a magazine, but because you've lived it, you know it, you're motivated, and you're out to make positive change. You know all the little pieces that have to happen in order to make headway on a problem. That's where your authentic, lived experience comes in. It's why you get up in the morning. It might be why you end up chairing a committee or even running for political office.

Your path as leader and change-maker won't be easy, but it will be *amazing*.

THE SUNDAY STAR

"WHERE THE SPIRIT OF THE LORD IS, THERE IS LIBERTY" 2 COR. 3:17

★ INDYSTAR
A GANNETT COMPANY

SUNDAY, MARCH 29, 2015 | CITY EDITION
AN EDITION OF THE INDIANAPOLIS STAR

'RELIGIOUS FREEDOM'

PENCE SEEKS TO CLARIFY LAW

State Rep. Christina Hale, D-Indianapolis, speaks in opposition of Indiana's recently passed Religious Freedom Restoration Act who gathered on the steps of the Indiana Statehouse on Saturday.

RFRA EXPLAINED

What the law really means for all Hoosiers

Stephanie Wang | stephanie.wang@indystar.com

Will Indiana's new religious freedom law really allow businesses to deny service to customers who are gay?

Will the law necessarily to protect persons from being forced into performing same-sex weddings?

Will it provide a legal rationale for Christian bakeries to refuse to make a cake for a same-sex couple's wedding?

The problem with these questions is that the answers depend on whom you ask — especially among those most emotionally involved, but even within the legal community. And now, with Gov. Mike Pence's announcement Saturday that he will seek further legislation to "clarify" the act, it could become even more complicated.

The argument over what Pence has thus signed becomes not only intellectual, but visceral, vicious, ugly. Both sides dig in, because each thinks the other is flatly wrong — in their hearts, and on the facts. And the debate rages on, sometimes spiraling to a place so far away from the law itself.

▶ See LAW, Page 12A

Gov. Mike Pence says he'll support legislation to clarify the intent of RFRA.

THOUSANDS RALLY
"We have it our state." "Fix the bill," vows among charity rowd. 3EA

ANGIE'S LIST HALTS EXPANSION
CEO says Gov. Pence "has got a blind spot on this (RFRA)." 12A

EDITORIAL: SWEAR, INDIANA.
A bad week sent a bad message about our state. Now it's time to heal. 19A

STAR EXCLUSIVE

Governor's team races to lessen the damage

Tim Swarens
Columnist

Gov. Mike Pence, overwhelmed by a fast-spreading political firestorm, told The Star on Saturday that he will support the introduction of legislation to "clarify" that Indiana's controversial Religious Freedom Restoration Act does not permit discrimination against gays and lesbians.

"I support religious liberty, and I support this law," Pence said in an exclusive interview. "But we are in discussion with legislative leaders this weekend to see if there's a way to clarify the intent of the law."

The governor, although not ready to provide details on what the new bill will say, said he expects the legislation to be introduced into the General Assembly this coming week.

Asked if that legislation might include making gay and lesbian Hoosiers a protected legal class, Pence said, "That's not on my agenda."

Amid the deepest crisis of his political career, Pence said

▶ See PENCE, Page 16A

That's JD Ford standing next to me. He had lost his race for Indiana Senate, but never stood down. He continued to show up, stay involved, and won his race the next time around. Now he is Senator Ford, the first out-of-the-closet LGBTQI+ member of the Indiana General Assembly. His voice is dearly needed. As is yours.

FIRST, THE BAD NEWS

Millennials may have been the last generation to have some semblance of a roadmap to life. Until recently, it was pretty much generally accepted that—at least in the United States and most developed countries—an education guaranteed a job. If you could get a high school degree or the equivalent, you were employable. If you could get a university degree, you would be on a path to success and financial reward. You'd be able to pay your bills, save a little money, do well by your children, and retire comfortably.

That is not the case anymore. That predictability—about avenues you could pursue to guarantee a secure adulthood—is a thing of the past. Generation Z and those who come after are facing a lot of anxiety and uncertainty. The employment landscape is changing, from manufacturing to retail, and young people are starting to have to deal with the impact of artificial intelligence. In fact, now is likely the most stressful time to be a young person in the history of the world. Even the nature of war is changing, and the burgeoning threats of cyberwarfare, biological warfare, and more, are very real. Does it feel like the future is looming down on you? If so, you're right—it is.

All of which is to say: **this journey is not always going to be easy.**

Keep your eyes on the prize. You're going to have a lot of life to live, and a lot of good things are going to happen to you—but it's going to take creativity and perseverance. Don't let yourself be fooled by adults looking back over their shoulder filled with nostalgia for the way things were when they were your age. Your path is going to be different, and probably harder—because of decisions made by those very same adults, who have passed the proverbial buck, the societal problems that they created, time and again along to you.

To find your happiness and purpose as a leader and change-maker will require hard work and discipline.

There's no sugarcoating it: you're going to inherit a lot of crap, the residue of countless bad decisions made out of self-interest, by people in power, from all political persuasions. It may sound harsh, but it's the truth. And nobody's talking about it.

It's not good enough. Not good enough for you, not good enough for me, not good enough for humanity—and it's beyond time for someone to *say it.*

This is why you're needed now more than ever. Not just to protest—though that is important too—but also to seek positions of power, to run for elected office, to step up as decision-makers, change-makers, and people who can actually do something about society's problems before it's too late. **The sad fact is that you're going to have to clean up a lot of the messes that are being made right now.**

Some of these messes are invisible...until they aren't, as people learned in Flint, Michigan, where it was discovered that the drinking water was contaminated. In your lifetime, there are going to be many more stories like that, maybe in your own communities. What are you going to do about it?

If not clean water, what will be your issue? Sadly, there is no shortage of problems out there that are desperately urgent and important, where you can make a big difference.

Why not you? (Warning: you're going to hear me say that a lot in this book.) Are you going to be the person to step up and make the change, or are you going to be like your elders who kicked the can down the road? I can't make this decision for you, but I can tell you that relying on someone else to save us—believing that others will somehow automatically emerge to solve our problems—is a dead end.

If not you, who? You have a good heart and a good mind. You're in it for the right reasons. It is up to you now to take on these responsibilities and challenge the status quo. What are you waiting for?

What will your issue be?

THE HARDEST TIME EVER IN MODERN HISTORY TO BE A YOUNG PERSON

J.D. Ford knew early on that he was different from other kids. As a youth, he didn't know what to do about the fact that he was into guys, not girls, but it wasn't really a problem until high school. That's when the bullying started.

There's nothing new, unfortunately, about teasing and bullying. Teenagers can be merciless when it comes to making fun of anyone who is different or out of step from the mainstream in any way. That was how it was when I was a teen, and it is still like that. Adolescence is hard for virtually everyone, but for some, it can be a real nightmare—and in many ways, it is even harder in today's world, where technology has amplified the scale of these problems.

While we have made great strides as a society in battling homophobia, our young people are arguably more susceptible than ever to harassment and worse. Cyber-bullying has emerged as one of the most devastating trends impacting youth over the past decade. Like so many others, J.D. was a victim of online bullying. It was rough. But not only did he make it through those difficult years, he also later found his calling as a State Senator fighting discrimination of all kinds. Today, he is the first openly gay person ever elected to Indiana's state legislature.

How did he do it? Both of his grandparents were elected officials. His maternal grandfather was a city councilman, and his dad's mom was a city auditor. In an interview with the *Zionsville Times Sentinel*, he credited them with inspiring his path: "When I was a little boy, I would go to the grocery store or bank and see neighbors and everyday people come up to them and say, 'Thank you for help on this issue.' I really felt that was such a cool and noble thing they were involved with."

Clearly, J.D. inherited his family's strong sense of civic duty and servant leadership. But that was only one piece of the puzzle. He knew what it felt like to be different, and he wanted to be a voice for others who felt different and left out in a variety of ways. J.D. also knew that he would have to create his own opportunities in life. His dad was a truck driver. His mom worked helping the elderly at a retirement home. He saw how they had to struggle just to keep the lights on and put food on the table. He wanted to make life better for them and others like them. He ended up sending himself to college and becoming the first person in his family to graduate from university. Later, he even went on to get his master's degree. But it wasn't enough. He knew he had to do something that would allow him to scale up and help not just ten people or twenty people but thousands. He realized the only way he could do that was by changing laws, particularly laws that discriminate against the most vulnerable communities.

After his historic win in the 2018 state election, he gave a stirring victory speech which included this remarkable line: "Every marginalized group—people of color, women, Muslims, Jewish Hoosiers, seniors, LGBTQ+ Hoosiers, just to name a few—you now have a voice in the Indiana General Assembly."

They certainly do.

TAPPED ON THE SHOULDER

J.D. had a tough time when he was younger, and maybe you did too. Maybe you're still in the thick of it. The truth is, most of us go through a lot of pain and heartache in our lives. There are those daggers to the heart again: **sometimes it feels like death by a thousand knives.** Or like everybody else is out there living fabulous lives—everybody except you. What you have to remember is that what people put on social media is not reality. It's an image of perfection that is constructed and manipulated.

When you see these images, you might think no one else has problems. But when you dig a little deeper and start connecting with people on a human level—when you have real conversations about what they're going through—you realize that everyone is struggling with *something*. And there are a lot more people out there dealing with the same issue that you care so much about. When you come to this understanding, it touches your life in a very personal way. You start to learn about other issues they need help with. You see that they just need someone to listen and hear their pain. But they also need someone to act—someone who's prepared to do something.

That someone can be you.

When you feel that pull, that's when you know that you've been tapped on the shoulder by something bigger and greater. You realize you're in a position to make the changes that are needed. You feel it. You've found your thing, your *why*. But this can only happen if you have positioned yourself to be able to act when the call for help comes.

The call *will* come.

Will you be ready? Will you be positioned to seize the moment? This is your time, your opportunity to scale up your potential for helping other people—folks who share your challenges but maybe aren't prepared to do something themselves.

Why you and not them? Sure, they might be prettier, smarter, more athletic, or have better "stuff." But they aren't you: they don't have your determination and passion and perspective. You've earned those the hard way, and that's exactly what will make you such a strong and effective change-maker for years to come.

No one person can see all and be all and understand all, which is why your angle—your insight into all that you have seen, felt, and experienced—is so critical. Literally, no one else has this particular power but you. What are you going to do with it?

Have you positioned yourself to act
when the call for help comes?

TURNING CHALLENGE INTO OPPORTUNITY

Yes, it's a very tough time to be a young person, and the problems we're facing as a society are real and profound. But the only way to confront them is with clear-eyed realism and a passion to deliver change. I take great inspiration from our history. There have been lots of times in the past when the future of our country, and the world, seemed incredibly bleak. We have been through world wars, depressions, terrorist attacks, and more. These challenges seemed unfathomable at the time, almost unendurable, and yet we not only survived them but went on to thrive and reach great heights.

We can do that again—but only if people like you step up and say, "It is up to me. I want to make that better future a reality."

The issues we face today are incredibly complex and costly, financially and otherwise. But there's a silver lining to everything. With challenge comes opportunity. Like in eras past, we can not only survive these difficult times but also innovate and see new breakthroughs that lead us to a better place as a society. We have all the potential in the world—the technology is certainly there—to bring about the changes we need, but it's not going to come without a great degree of hard work and sacrifice.

That's been the case through our history, and now is no different. Especially during periods of challenge and even, sometimes, catastrophic events, **it comes down to leaders like you.**

Is your hair on fire yet?

How are you going to step into your role as changemaker? What is your issue? For me, it was sexual assault.

For you, it could be anything—even maybe a crisis that's not on most of our radars yet, like how we would respond if our power grid were taken out by cyber-terrorists. There is no shortage, sadly, of new threats to our safety and well-being. But we have faced threats before—in the '60s, the Cuban Missile Crisis brought us closer than we've ever been, before or after, to global nuclear war—and we overcame them, at least in the short term.

By no means am I suggesting we be sanguine or blasé about the severity of our twenty-first century challenges. They are as vast as they are extreme. But I *am* calling upon you to confront these issues with all the strength and courage you have in you.

You may not realize yet just how powerful and resilient you are—how much you can change the world. You may not see it until life tests you in a major way. For me, it didn't happen until I experienced my darkest moment early in life, when I became pregnant and life changed forever.

Places to go and people to see: here, Owen and I are both heading to school. These weren't easy times, but I learned firsthand how childcare, education, and opportunity are necessary to achieve the American Dream...and that I needed to fight for everyone to have their chance, too.

THE "WORST THING" MIGHT JUST SAVE YOUR LIFE

I t was the worst thing to ever happen to me. That's what I thought: that my life was over, unrecoverable. I was only nineteen. A college student. Not married. It was an unplanned pregnancy (I'll spare you the details), and I didn't know what to do. I was terrified. Didn't have a plan. All I knew was I had to raise this little kid; that was my new reality. I dropped out of college.

Let me tell you, there is nothing like the pure terror you feel when you take a home pregnancy test. On the box, it says it takes five minutes to get a result. Well, it doesn't take five minutes. It takes about five *seconds* for that plus sign to shine bright in your face. And then, all of a sudden, like that, your world is completely different.

My brothers both reacted to the news—separately, and in their own ways—by saying, basically, "Face it, Christie. You're always going to be a loser now." Hard words to hear, and I believed them. For about three minutes. But they were three very difficult minutes. I knew I had no choice but to step up and go to work and hustle to make sure my baby would be taken care of. It was that simple: sometimes life doesn't go as planned.

In retrospect, my pregnancy—and its consequences— wasn't the worst thing at all. In fact, it turned out to be one of the best. But I wouldn't know that for some time down the road. And neither will you, when the "worst thing" possible happens to you, whatever that thing may be. It won't be easy, it won't be fun, but **it might just end up saving your life**. I know it saved mine. It helped me find my strength. What seemed like an ending for me was really a new beginning.

As you'll see in this chapter, we all have these life-chang- ing moments. The key is to harness the moment, no matter how bad or dark, toward growing and evolving—and helping others.

> *"Face it, Christie. You're always*
> *going to be a loser now."*

WHEN LIFE TAKES A U-TURN

Look, everyone is different, and your life may go along just as you always expected and planned for, with no major bumps in the road. It's possible. But mine certainly didn't. Instead, it took a big U-turn when I was nineteen. The important point is that when you come to that screeching turning point in your life, *if* you come to it, you try to see the bigger picture: that no matter how devastating it may feel at the time, your "worst thing" is actually an opportunity for reinvention. In fact, it can be the very thing that gives you the motivation and power, the steel, to step up your game in this crazy game of life.

I know it sounds counterintuitive, but these heart-wrenching, life-challenging moments will ultimately be the fuel you use to do all the greater, bolder things you couldn't have even imagined up to this point.

You couldn't imagine because you couldn't relate. It hadn't happened to you; you hadn't felt it; you didn't know. But now you do.

Or you will, later. And therein lies the rub. Often, as was the case with me, it takes many years to be able to look back and see how your "worst thing" saved your life. You can't see it happening while the events are unfolding. It's one of the cruel ironies of being human. You can't Monday-morning-quarterback your life while you're playing in the Big Game on Sunday. Just know that one day, you *will* see it. The important thing for now is that you're in the game and you're playing.

The revelation that the worst thing had actually saved his life certainly didn't come immediately to Jay Ruckelshaus, one of the young people you need to hear about. But when it did, he became stronger and more effective—as an individual *and* a change-maker for the greater good—than ever before.

Jay was a popular high school student. You know, he was *that* kid: happy, social, got good grades. It seemed like everything was going his way until one summer afternoon when he went swimming with friends. He dove in the reservoir, misjudged the depth, and broke his neck. Woke up days later a paraplegic, his life forever changed. He went from being a high school sports star, a handsome, smart kid who had it all, to not being able to walk or feed or take care of himself on the most basic level. He had no choice but to completely start over.

It was beyond humbling, and it could have been the end of everything. Not only physically. When someone suffers a personal tragedy on such a level—one which most of us can't even imagine—it is tempting and understandable for them to just give up mentally and emotionally, to decide, *That's it, I've had enough.*

But then you hear about people like Jay who refuse to let go of hope, even though they have good reason to. Instead, they say, "No, that's not going to be me. I'm not going to be a statistic and lose this game of life." How do they do it? How do they summon the courage?

Jay worked harder than anyone he knew at rehab. He was there for many, many months. After finally returning to school in a wheelchair and slowly getting his confidence back, **he began to realize there was so much more now that he could and should be doing for other people.** It was the beginning of a calling to service. He knew he wanted to go to college and had in fact already gotten admitted to

Duke University on a full scholarship, but there were so many open questions. Was it even possible for him physically to go to college by himself? Jay lived in Indiana and Duke was hundreds of miles away in North Carolina. Who would help him? How would he be able to do the schoolwork without use of his hands?

Not only did he overcome these challenges and go to the college he had long dreamed of, but he also started a foundation for other young people with disabilities, specifically those who have suffered similar spinal cord injuries but don't have his financial advantages. Jay's foundation is called Ramp Less Traveled and is devoted to spreading the message that college is indeed attainable for students with these disabilities.

After graduating valedictorian from his high school and then from Duke, *summa cum laude* no less, Jay was awarded a Rhodes scholarship (one of only two students at Duke to receive it) to study at Oxford. Watch for him: Jay will not stop using his voice, and you can bet he will continue to take on roles that position him to effect action on the issues he cares about.

YOUR GREATEST CHALLENGE IS
YOUR GREATEST STRENGTH

What are we to make of Jay and his incredible story? His "worst thing" was bad, no doubt about that. But remarkably, instead of giving up, or being angry at the world, he was able—not immediately but with time—to come to a new perspective. He saw that there were others out there like him who needed help, who were paraplegic and trying to go to college but couldn't without financial assistance. There were also those who weren't as lucky as him to have family support and who couldn't afford to hire caregivers.

Jay is a true hero, and he was even invited to tell his story on the *Today* show. But his story is far from over, and it's not going to be easy. He is going to live the rest of his life in a wheelchair. There are a lot of things he's still going to have to figure out and work hard to overcome. But critically, he has developed the strength and resilience to tackle new challenges ahead. Moreover, he's developed a passion to channel his power toward helping others. He used his opportunity to go on national TV to speak on behalf, and for the greater good, of others like him.

I would not be surprised at all to see Jay become the first paraplegic governor of his home state. Or even a US President! What's more: he won't be ashamed or embarrassed about being in a wheelchair. It won't be something he asks the Press Corps to hide—like FDR famously did with the debilitating effects of his polio.

Jay will know that his greatest challenge is actually his greatest strength because it is what allows him to inspire and impact others.

Wherever his path may take him, Jay is moving ahead, forward, and positioning himself for new opportunities in life. He still suffers the consequences of the tragic day when he had his diving accident, but he's using the strength he gained from it to accomplish great things, for himself and others.

You can scale your life up as well. Don't think for a minute you can't.

Again, it may not happen right away. And you may not come to these insights until long after *your* "worst thing" happens. I encourage you to take the long view. Remember that being a leader, advocate, and change-maker is a *lifelong* project. There are going to be ups and downs, twists and turns.

But don't be surprised when what you thought was the end of your life turns out to be the very thing that saves you and fuels your advocacy for years to come.

Being a leader and change-maker is a lifelong effort.

It takes so many people to help you get over the finish line. It feels like a miracle when people step up to help you, but if you are in it for the right reasons, they will.

3

IT'S ALL
ABOUT YOU...
EXCEPT IT ISN'T

When Mohammed Osman Mohammed first came to this country, he moved into what a lot of people would think is a crummy apartment. But to him, it was the most luxurious residence he could ever imagine. For the first time in his life, he had a place of his own, where he could be alone: his own sink and toilet, a bed to lie down on whenever he wanted. When it was cold, he could turn on the heat, and when it was hot, he could turn on the air conditioning. **Having spent most of his adult life in the world's largest refugee camp, he took nothing for granted.**

Mohammed grew up in Somalia, where he herded goats and camels. He was only five years old when he lost his mother. By age nine, he had run away to the city during wartime, and by eleven, was an orphan, having lost his father to the violence of civil war. He finally escaped across the border to Kenya, where he lived in the crowded camp all those years, in a place called Dadaab.

Then, by virtue of sheer luck, he was plucked out and given an opportunity to come to the United States and make a new life for himself in Indianapolis.

Mohammad's brother, who had polio, was not so lucky. Why did Mohammed enjoy this great fortune when his brother didn't? The question nagged at him. *Why me?* He struggled with guilt and thought often not just of his brother but the literally hundreds of thousands of people he had left behind at the camp.

Before coming to the United States, Mohammed had never really had any possessions at all, nothing that he could call his own. Here, on the other hand, he had been given—through the organization that had sponsored him—everything from the clothes on his back to the shoes on his feet, from the food in his kitchen to the miraculous refrigerator he stored it all in.

He knew he'd been dealt an opportunity he couldn't squander. It wasn't his to waste. He owed it to his family, his brother. But here he was now in this strange land where he didn't even speak the language. On top of that, he had very little formal education. He knew he had to roll up his sleeves, learn English, and get to work, not only academically but also so he could support himself. He didn't have any safety net of family in America. He would have to do it all himself.

Not only did Mohammed send himself through school, working toward a finance degree from Indiana University, he also went and studied in England. When he returned, I tried to help him find his first job as a college graduate. I introduced him to a bunch of people, set up coffee meetings for him. Eventually, he got a job in the finance department of Eli Lilly. It was not intended to be a permanent position. It was a six-month contract job, but they were so impressed with him that they ended up creating a job from scratch for him in their Corporate Social Responsibility department.

Not only was Mohammed driven by a desire to give back to his family but also by a deeper call to service to help others. These days, he does humanitarian work in Africa and speaks publicly about issues facing refugees from many troubled regions of the world.

But he struggled at first to put himself out there.

Even he—someone who had walked the walk and lived through so much—had a hard time allowing himself to step into his role as a public voice on these important subjects. Shy by nature, he avoided the limelight.

Eventually, however, the call to serve became too powerful to hold back, and he did what he knew was right: used his story and his experience to help and inspire others.

Don't let your humility get in the way of helping others.

MODESTY DOESN'T SAVE LIVES

When the opportunity arises to take up the noble calling to serve and to speak out for what's right, it's no time for modesty. You must step into your bold new role with confidence. It's not being arrogant. In fact, it's the opposite. If not for you, the task wouldn't get done. More to the point, at the end of the day, **it's not about you—it's about the results.**

To be a truly effective leader, you can't be hesitant to use all your talent at hand. Embrace your courage and righteousness and use it to help others. If anything, it's selfish to *deny* the world your unique perspective and gifts. Imagine if Mohammed had done that!

As I like to put it, "It's all about you...except it isn't." Here's what I mean...

Yes, it's all about you, in that you're the one whose reputation is on the line in this life of being a leader and change-maker. You're the one who has to get up early and do the work. You're the one who has to perform the heavy lifting to bring about the change you are working toward. You're the one who has to know your topic better than anyone else, care about it more than anyone else, and be more articulate and persuasive than anyone else.

In order to do that, inevitably there will be an element of self-promotion. You'll need to build up your personal profile so that others can connect with you and hear your message.

That comes easier to some people than others. If you're like Mohammed, it's not your natural way of being. And of course, you don't want to come across as vain, so you should always self-police against that tendency. However, it is also **necessary to let people know who you are.** In today's world, and with social media, to a certain extent we all portray ourselves and are seen by others—like it or not— as a personal brand.

This isn't bad or egotistical in itself. The key is to craft a brand for yourself as a change-maker who wants to do good for others. In order to do this well, you have to tell your story in a public way—one that comes with some necessary risks.

You're the one who has to know your topic better than anyone else, care about it more than anyone else, and be more articulate and persuasive than anyone else.

BRANDING YOURSELF TO EFFECT CHANGE

Every time you put yourself out there, you're going to get a lot of "likes." We all know that feels good. But what about when you encounter the trolls and haters? They are coming your way as well. You have to be prepared for it. Yes, you're going to be challenged. **People are going to say unflattering things about you. They're going to tell you you're not good enough, not sincere enough, that you don't know what you're talking about.** For better or worse, this is the nature of social media.

I've had to learn the hard way to never read the comments when I publish an article. Even with something seemingly as right and noble as the fight against sexual violence, there are a lot of different opinions out there, and it's okay when they don't align with mine. What is *not* okay is when attacks get personal. Having an exchange of ideas is healthy, but all too often, we see how vitriolic and even violent threats can get online.

Especially on the internet, where you're not face-to-face, people don't hold back from saying things that are really hurtful. Sometimes they also imagine or project thoughts onto you that are not true or accurate to what you really believe. But the average person reading a comment doesn't know that. They don't know you. They have no idea.

All of which is to say, when you put yourself out there publicly, you're making yourself vulnerable. You're setting yourself up to be even more susceptible to criticism. Sometimes it comes from people you don't expect either. In a way, it's easier to take when it's online and coming from a stranger. What about when it comes from those who are closest to you, from your nearest and dearest?

You have to have a thick skin. But more than that, you have to keep a certain perspective. And this is where the second part of "It's All About You...Except It Isn't" comes in. The message of that second phrase is, essentially, *sticks and stones may break your bones, but what matters are the results, the people you're fighting for.*

In order to be an effective change-maker, you have to learn to embrace that mentality. What you're doing—in putting yourself out there, on the public stage—is worth it, even if it makes you look like you're "trying to be *all that.*" It's worth it for the people you're helping.

Remember, you're not selling *yourself.* This isn't your favorite online influencer or sales-lebrity. You're using your unique gifts—your charisma, your passion—to help others. You're not doing it for you. You're doing it because the people coming along behind you *need* this critical change to happen.

Again, it's about **positional leadership.** It's not enough to be the person on the sidelines saying, "Hey, pay attention to this." You have to empower yourself to actually do something about it. Don't squander your opportunity. Just like with Mohammed, it's not your opportunity to waste.

Chances are you have lived a very different life than Mohammed. But in some ways, you have just as much at stake. One thing we know for certain: this is the only life you get.

So, don't let the moments slip by, and **don't let your self-perceived inadequacies stand in the way of making your mark on the world.**

Don't listen to the haters who think you're trying to be all that.

YOUR TURN TO ACT

When you're positioned to do something for others—when you are a decision-maker and something important comes up on your watch—it's time to stop worrying about how you may look to others and just take action. Even if it's not your issue, you know what the right thing is to do. You understand what's at stake for people. It's your turn to make change happen.

Now here's the downside: if you're *not* preparing, not listening, if your eyes aren't open and you're not paying attention—and especially, if you're hoarding your talents, sitting on them, sitting on your hands on the sidelines— then you're not going to be able to act when the moment calls for it. You won't deliver the change that people desperately need. In fact, it's not an exaggeration to say that **people will be worse off for your inaction.**

Think of the students who spoke out after the tragic Parkland shootings. When they started school that Fall, they didn't think they'd finish their year on the cover of *Time* magazine. They were just looking forward to an average year of high school.

We all know what happened next: a violent teen walked in and took the lives of their friends and teachers. Then, in the aftermath of the horrific tragedy, these survivors—stricken with grief and anger—decided enough was enough. They took it upon themselves to do something about it, to speak out.

They were just regular young people who cared. They certainly weren't vain self-promoters. But they used the media to promote themselves and their cause so that they could amplify their reach and make a bigger impact.

And they didn't stop to ask, "Who am I to be speaking out when there are all these adults in the room who probably know better?"

State Rep. Chris Chyung, State Rep. Mara Candelaria Reardon, and State Rep. Earl Harris gathered to support the Indiana Latino Legislative Fellow program. I was only the fourth person of Latinx heritage to be elected to the state assembly. Mara was the third (and first Latina!), and Earl the fifth. Chris Chyung was only the second Asian American, and the youngest serving member during his term. Government will be stronger when elected officials better reflect our communities.

DON'T BE SO SURE ABOUT THOSE "ADULTS IN CHARGE"

fter I became pregnant and dropped out of college, after my brothers made me feel I was destined to be a loser forever, I had a powerful realization. Instead of giving up, I came to recognize that if I was really such a loser, **the so-called adults didn't exactly have it all together either.**

In retrospect, I'm glad my brothers reacted like they did. They were disappointed in me, and their words were hard to hear—but I needed to hear them at the time. This helped me begin to see more clearly what life was like for people in my situation and how much better it could and should be. Wherever you stand on the issue of reproductive justice, I think most everyone will agree that we have to do a better job by the children who are born and who need all kinds of support.

When I got pregnant, I saw that society wasn't set up very well to do right by little kids. The data and evidence are clear: young people do better when they are in quality preschools, when they're taught to read, write, count. Getting pregnant at age nineteen made me aware of all the bad decisions made by the powers-that-be, decisions that made it harder to succeed, and made life worse, not better, for families and children.

There was a lot of bad, a lot that needed to be fixed. The adults in charge, at least in my community, hadn't really done the work to support the lives of our young children.

This was a shock to me but also an important turning point. We all expect the adults to have it figured out and to be making all the right decisions, for the right reasons. But that turns out to be far from the reality.

In the eyes of my brothers, now that I was a teen mom, that was all that I could ever be or become. But my brothers weren't the real problem. They were just channeling what society dictated. **But who made these rules anyway?**

I was pretty angry at the time. It still makes me angry. We have these perceptions of what success looks like, and it doesn't look like someone who's nineteen and pregnant.

If that made me a loser, what did a winner look like in our society? Would I be a winner if I lived a traditional life exactly like our mother? Did success mean I needed to become a nurse, or a teacher, and get married, or be a stay-at-home mom? Looking back, I understand that my brothers meant well, but their criticism was pointed in the wrong direction.

I knew then, and I know now, that if I was such a loser, the adults in charge—the "successful" ones who we were supposed to look up to—didn't seem like they were doing a very good job either.

How skewed is it anyway that just because I became pregnant, it was now a given that my life would be over before it began? I rejected that thinking. It just wasn't acceptable to me that my destiny now was to be stuck in a cycle of poverty and lack of opportunity. It wasn't right that simply because my life had started out with a different cadence than my peers, I could never become something better, or fulfill my hopes and dreams.

I wasn't going to stand for it.

In the years that followed, I went to work. I took any job that paid our bills, including childcare, tuition, food, gas, and healthcare. It was so hard, but I managed to get back in school and, eventually, became a Rotary International Ambassadorial Fellow and earned my university degree.

Who made the rules anyway?

NEWSFLASH: THE ADULTS HAVEN'T FIGURED IT ALL OUT EITHER

Sad to say, but the grown-ups in charge are flying by the seat of their pants just like you are. There is no manual to life. Adults may have wrinkles and gray hair, but they're just like teenagers in so many ways.

Not only that, but many of those adults in positions of power and wealth are definitely not in it for the right reasons. Why do we assume they are? Be careful of projecting your own noble motivations onto others. It's in our nature as humans to do this. **When we think we know somebody, we assign our own good intentions and feelings onto them— whether they deserve it or not.** But there are some people who are just selfish and greedy. These individuals are going to come in and out of our lives, and it won't always be obvious to us in the moment. We won't see their true colors at first.

We may end up dating them, or they may become our best frenemy. It could take a while for us to figure out that they're really in it for themselves, or whatever negative agenda fuels them. Maybe they're lazy and self-interested. Maybe they just don't care.

The difference is that *you do care.*

You *are* in it for the right reasons, and that is a precious, important thing. You must cultivate and grow it and improve that power within you.

Back in the '60s, people used to say, "You shouldn't trust anyone over the age of thirty." That's taking it a bit far. Certainly, the value of respecting your elders and learning from them remains an important one. But equally, if not more, important is to **question and challenge the established wisdom of previous generations.**

Adults are just old teenagers.

It's up to you now to be intentional about the cultivation of your own wisdom and motivation, so that you can work in a meaningful way sooner. Most of us won't. But you will. You may be one of a small tribe. Many of your contemporaries, even many of your friends, are going to become adults who sleepwalk their way through life and resign themselves to the status quo. They'll decide, *Well, this is the way it is, and it's the way it's always going to be.*

Don't let that be you.

Being intentional about getting yourself prepared—and cultivating your own wisdom now—means you are empowering yourself today to be an effective change-maker tomorrow.

LIFE IS ONLY AS FAIR AS YOU MAKE IT

When you look around your own environment—your school, your neighborhood—you probably see things that are just plain wrong. You see people suffering and being treated unfairly every day.

The sad fact is that it doesn't necessarily get that much better. Not without people fighting to make it better. People like you. There's this myth that life is fair. But it's not really true, no matter what phase of life you're in. Still, the myth is so ingrained in us, so deeply embedded in society, that it's hard to see things for how they really are. We think life will work out the right way in the end, and for the right reasons. But it won't—at least not on its own. Not unless we make it work out that way.

It gets better...but only if you make it better.

One of the schools in my statehouse district—Lawrence North High School—ran a secret food pantry on Fridays because there were so many teens that didn't have enough food at home to eat. This is in a wealthy urban/suburban neighborhood, but not everyone who goes to school there is wealthy. Some students don't have enough food to sustain them over the weekend, so they're given—discretely— backpacks full of food.

There are young people going hungry all over our country. I promise you there are students you know right now who have this problem too. It's a terrible, terrible situation because if you don't eat, as a teenager, it has a direct impact on your ability to learn in school. At that age, your brain is continuing to grow. These are critical years, and nutrition is so important.

Worse, there are teenagers who should be getting help and who could but aren't because of the stigma attached to hunger.

It doesn't have to be this way. There are solutions.

I bring it up because it's an example of a terrible problem that's happening right now in our backyards—all of our backyards—because of the bad decisions made by adults. But it's also an example of young people doing something about it. It was the students themselves at Lawrence North who came up with the idea for the secret food pantry. **They figured they had to take action. Otherwise, their friends wouldn't eat.**

The adults had the resources, the food. But they didn't know how to make the program a reality because they were disconnected from the daily lives of the kids. They didn't understand the embarrassment and shame that came with admitting you needed this kind of help. They weren't thinking about it through the lens of the child him- or herself. But the *peers* of the program's beneficiaries understood and figured out a way that it could work, while respecting the privacy of the students receiving the aid.

This groundbreaking program has now been embraced by the school's administration, and its success is being replicated at other schools throughout the region.

Sometimes it's young people who are able to come up with the fresh ideas and solutions that the adults can't.

It's why your voice and insight are so important—especially in today's ever-accelerating world, where the ability to be nimble and forecast and react to new situations and circumstances is so vital.

Mayor Pete and me talking about the issues of the day with Central Indiana community leaders at the home of Dr. Ajay and Dr. Padma Ponugoti and their daughters. Photo provided by Ajay Ponugoti.

THE BATMAN
PRINCIPLE

Some say this story is an urban legend, but I was taken with it nonetheless. It's about the actor Christian Bale. At a certain point in his career, he was terrified that he had peaked early, that his best days had come and gone. At a young age, he had won a coveted role in one of Stephen Spielberg's masterworks, 1987's *Empire of the Sun*. It was the gig of a lifetime—and hard to top, particularly for a child actor.

As anyone who's watched a Hollywood biopic or two knows, when a child actor grows up a bit and the jobs start drying up, they start to question themselves. Maybe they are going through an awkward adolescence. They wonder whether lightning will ever strike twice. They yearn to be able to drive their career toward the kind of enduring success that's going to sustain them over time.

Urban legend has it that Christian Bale became convinced he had to win the role of Robin alongside George Clooney's Batman in the much-anticipated sequel to *Batman Forever*. He just knew that it would be the thing to restart his career and help him make the kind of impact over time that he always dreamed of.

But a lot of other talented people read for the Robin part, and ultimately, Christian Bale was *not* selected for the role. It went to another Chris: Christopher O'Donnell.

A sad turn of events for Bale, but what neither he nor anyone could have predicted at the time—and what is all too common now—is that reboots of superhero franchises would become a huge trend. In fact, Bale himself would go on to play Batman in a reboot of the series, for Christopher Nolan's *The Dark Knight* trilogy. These films were hugely successful at the box office and became a cultural phenomenon.

Ironically, if Bale had won the role years earlier as Robin, it would have been impossible for him to be cast later in the lead as Batman. Of course, he had no way of knowing that; it wasn't something he could have planned for. At the time, it wouldn't have even been in the realm of possibility. But there it was. It happened. And it happened *because* he failed. If he had not lost out the first time, he would have been ineligible for the role that renewed his career and ensured his place as an A-list Hollywood star forever more.

It's like that for all of us. **We can't always imagine what that next opportunity around the corner might be because we can't see it.** We convince ourselves that we have it all figured out and that we're in control of the universe and know what path we're on. But the truth is, we can't predict all the myriad opportunities in life. There are so many different possibilities that could come in so many different ways, through friendships and connections, or just by being in the right place at the right time.

We think we have this rock-solid, bulletproof logic or rationale behind why we do the things we do or how we are going to get to the next stage in our career. But it doesn't usually work that way, and that is definitely true when it comes to a life of service, as a leader, advocate, and change-maker.

LETTING GO OF THE
"ONE WAY FORWARD" MENTALITY

In all the work I've done with young people over the years, I've seen how the ones who are making the biggest difference in the world today—and poised to become the exciting leaders of tomorrow—didn't actually set out for this to be their destiny.

But crucially, they opened themselves up to it.

We all get hung up sometimes on making sure thing go "according to plan." We tell ourselves we *have* to land this particular internship or job. "If I don't get into Harvard, my life is over," we say. "It will never work out!" Yes, it will. You just have to let go of having your heart set on the one way forward. There are many paths. Life is like water: it finds a way. A stream will find its direction.

You have a future, and it will eventually unfold. Much of it may still be a mystery, and that's okay. Don't give up if you don't get such-and-such job or scholarship. Christian Bale didn't give up after he lost the role of Robin. He continued to go out on auditions. And what came back to him eventually turned out to be something beyond his wildest dreams. He will forever be remembered for that role as Batman.

Life is like water: it finds a way.

Of course, none of this means that you should just sit back and let life happen *to* you. Especially **as a change-maker, you have to always be on the hunt, looking for openings and opportunities.** They're out there. They may be small and incremental, but you never know where they will lead. By working in the trenches on the issue that you care about, you will make valuable connections and also learn something about yourself, your motivation, your why that propels you and gives you the willpower to keep going.

At the end of the day, it's not about you. It's about the *issue* and the people you're helping. You may be spending more time than you'd like on things that don't feel like "success," but don't be so sure. By doing the hard often-unglamorous work and knowing your issue inside and out, you are preparing yourself—so that when you *are* finally in a place of positional power and advocacy, you will be ready. You'll have your facts right. You'll possess a depth of knowledge that comes from not only understanding the broader policy implications of whatever your issue may be but also spending time talking to people and hearing the lived experiences of those who have been negatively impacted.

Because you were open to different experiences when it counted, now you are able to be all the clearer and more specific about what you are trying to accomplish, as you stay active in the field.

Point is: sometimes the pathway to effective advocacy happens not because you've located yourself at some obvious choice like a school, internship, or volunteer opportunity. **Sometimes the best place to be is right where you are, doing the thing that you care most about.**

OPENING YOURSELF TO THE UNIVERSE

Pete Buttigieg is living proof that a circuitous route can sometimes be the *best* path to leadership. I've known Pete for a long time and believe that he represents exactly the kind of boldness—audacity, even—that we need right now. How's that? Most of you probably came to hear about Pete when, as the young mayor of South Bend, he ran for President of the United States. He did not win the presidency, of course, nor the democratic primary. But the point is: he went for it. And now he serves in the cabinet as Secretary of Transportation and one of President Biden's closest advisors.

His particular trajectory has never been seen before. Nothing like it, in fact. Was it audacious to run for president as a small-town mayor? Of course. But these are times that call for that kind of audacity—time for people like *you* to stand up in the same bold spirit and claim your strengths.

A circuitous route can sometimes be
the best path to leadership.

Pete won the Iowa primary! Yet, after a rollercoaster campaign, the time came when, after falling far behind, he made the wise decision to drop out of the race. So, what did he do next? Pete never stopped moving forward. He didn't give up but instead looked for the *next* opportunity to serve. He may not have been our country's expert on all things transportation. But he was in it for the right reasons and knew that he could do a great job as cabinet secretary. In leading a municipality in the middle of the Rust Belt, he had certainly learned firsthand the importance of transport and all its modes. But what really made the difference was how he took those lessons and that work ethic and pursued an ambitious goal of positional leadership in the executive branch of the federal government, trusting in himself and knowing he had the best interest of all Americans at heart.

It's a running theme for Pete: he steps up to take on a challenge that people initially scoff at and turns out to be remarkably competitive. He also knows how to build an unusually strong team. He did it when he ran for mayor and again when he ran for president.

Even more to the point, he doesn't let it bring him down when he loses. And he didn't just lose the *one* time. In fact, he lost again and again: first his race for State Treasurer, then when he was beaten by Tom Perez for Chair of the Democratic National Committee, and finally of course his presidential campaign. When that last one didn't work out, even though he never *planned* to become Secretary of Transportation, he saw an opportunity there and took it.

He got to play Batman, so to speak, on the president's cabinet.

I've watched Pete's career from the time I first met him when he was running for State Treasurer. He ran statewide, went to every county, shook countless hands, and invested so much of himself in order to show people that they could trust him as the chief guardian of their state's finances. It was a daunting task and disheartening when he lost. But then again, if he had succeeded, he might still be in that role of State Treasurer today, meaning he would have never run for chair of the DNC, mayor of South Bend, or President of the United States. He certainly wouldn't be serving as cabinet secretary.

Life has a way of revealing our true purpose in the end, and no one exemplifies this more than Pete Buttigieg.

LIVING WITHOUT A ROADMAP

None of us gets a roadmap to life. In fact, the more you learn about people, the more you realize they likely have the same fears and worries going on in their head that you have right now. They've all had trouble paying the bills at some point in their lives. They've all worried about their adequacy. And they've questioned, "Why didn't I get that opportunity? Why didn't I get that job? How do I double down?"

All I can say is that it's a liberating feeling when you realize that you're not in charge of the universe and, really, you're only guessing about what might make you happy in the future. It's a truth that can set you free.

Open yourself up to the universe, and you will find
your own "leading role" eventually.

Let go of seeing only one way forward.

Kicking off my campaign for Lieutenant Governor of the State of Indiana as the first former single mom and Latina to do so.

THE STICKY
PRINCIPLE

Sometimes in life, you know what you want to do in the big-picture scheme of things—you know what you care about and where you want to make an impact—but you just don't know how to go about doing it. The path is not clear.

From the time I was a young teen, I knew which issues I cared about most. I knew I wanted to help people and scale up my positive impact—but I didn't know how. Honestly, **I didn't think I was leader material. I questioned whether I was worthy enough to represent other people.** I never even thought to ask myself, *Why not me?* I had already assumed there would be others, who were smarter, better, etc., and would come along and take on the important issues I cared about as their own. The sad fact is nobody did.

Deep down, I suppose I knew I had to be ready and able to say yes if ever I *did* find that opportunity to be an effective change-maker. It was just hard to wrap my head around what the opportunity might be—until it became all too obvious.

It wasn't my idea. I wish I could say it was, but it came from a friend. I got a text message from her asking if I wanted to come over that Sunday to watch football and eat chili. I wrote back, "Can't this weekend."

Then, she asked me, "Hey, would you want to run for state representative?"

Without thinking twice, I texted back, "Hahaha."

But then, after I put the phone down, the idea stuck with me. *Well,* I thought, *maybe it's not totally crazy.* I picked up my phone again and googled the woman who was to become my opponent. The more I thought about it, the more I realized there was a synergy, an intersection between all the issues I cared about and this position that I would be ultimately competing for, to be a decision-maker in the general assembly. I also learned that my opponent did *not* stand for some of the things that I found to be critical when it came to helping people in the areas I cared most about.

In fact, sometimes she contributed to the problems I was trying to fix. For example, it made me want to set my hair on fire that in my state—in the twenty-first century!—women were being arrested for public indecency for breastfeeding. To me, that was unconscionable. I discovered that my opponent had voted against a bill to decriminalize breastfeeding. In fact, she had voted against it twice. Then, I began to dig a little deeper. The more I learned, the more motivated I became.

This opportunity was right in my sweet spot: the intersection of heart (my passion for all the issues I cared about most) and head (my skillset). I was getting fired up, and it was becoming easier by the day to believe in my own ability to drive change effectively. I would lie awake at night thinking about all the goals I would pursue as a representative in the state assembly and how I would accomplish what I needed to get done in order to be successful.

So, I surprised myself and ran for office. And then I surprised myself again by winning!

For the next four years, I represented a district of about 75,000 people in the Indiana General Assembly—a place where laws get made, laws that impact everything from how many days and hours you have to spend in school to how to prosecute criminals who traffic humans. But I would have never had the chance to serve in the assembly were it not for my good friend Robin, the one who had texted me on that fateful day. Robin and I had met through work. She and her husband Kip both knew my issues, my work, what I had been doing—how I had dedicated my career to supporting youth around the world in different ways—and saw that I was now in the right place at the right time to make a difference. It was just a matter of helping *me* see that.

Suddenly, I felt more alive than ever before. My first time running for office wasn't something I had actively sought. But it certainly wasn't like I was sitting around waiting to be discovered, or like Robin and Kip plucked me from thin air. Far from it. Rather, by having *put myself out there* in different ways, I was ready to strike when the stars aligned.

I had made myself "sticky," through hard work, intention, and all the life experiences I had sought—experiences that had contributed not only to the development of my character and values but also my skillset and know-how. I had never stopped immersing myself in the advocacy I cared so much about, specifically around sexual assault.

In fact, I could trace my path back to my experience with my friend Gabby all those years ago. Because of what happened that summer and how it changed me and opened up my consciousness, I had stayed active in that space ever since. I had done things like: mentoring and connecting victims of assault with the services they needed; arranging reciprocal babysitting opportunities for single moms; and volunteering as a CASA (Court Appointed Special Advocate) for kids and young people in court—often in harrowing abuse cases—for children who had no one else to represent their interests.

This was the stuff I cared most about. But I also knew it was all leading me *somewhere*, and one day I'd find a special opportunity to make my true impact.

So, when it did, **I ran with it and never looked back.**

How are you making yourself "sticky"?

THE IMPORTANCE OF SHOWING UP

Things do happen. Times change. New opportunities present themselves. Sometimes it's sheer luck. Or *chutzpah*.

But being open to the twists and turns of life *doesn't* mean just waiting to be discovered. This may seem obvious, but you have to actually show up. Being in the right place at the right time is all about setting yourself up to intersect with opportunity.

For me, both formally and informally, I made sure I was always out there, getting known as someone who cared about these issues, particularly ones impacting the lives of girls and women. People knew of my work as a mentor from the time before I was a legislator, when I first went to work for a global organization of volunteers dedicated to "serving the children of the world." The group is called Kiwanis International, and its members help kids *where they are*, in eighty different countries around the world—as well as network to fight significant problems that impact kids everywhere. For example, one of Kiwanis International's achievements is saving the developing world billions and billions of IQ points over time by ensuring that all people have iodine (a micronutrient, but one that was all people needed to develop intellectually) in their diet.

I was proud to be part of such a venerable organization as Kiwanis—and one whose work fit right in with the issues I cared about and the work that I've done throughout my life. In a similar vein to their iodine project, I helped launch a campaign to combat maternal and neonatal tetanus. The tragic thing about this disease—which has been found in humans for thousands of years and has even been referred to in ancient sacred texts as the Seven Day Disease—is that a perfectly healthy baby is fated to a horrible death, merely because the umbilical cord is cut with a dirty piece of metal or bamboo. In the days following the birth, the baby becomes increasingly distressed, unable to handle light, sound, or even a parent's touch, and ultimately dies in pain.

Even more tragically, it's a completely avoidable situation. You can give the mother, proactively, a vaccine that allows her to pass along the protection to the baby. And of course, you can educate people about how to sterilize the tools they use for cutting the cord. In recent years, much progress has been made around the world toward eliminating tetanus, but it's still a problem in many countries where women are not able to access adequate medical care.

Because I was involved with efforts like this, working in these critical ways to save lives around the world, it wasn't such a stretch to imagine me bringing this kind of solution-oriented mindset to the issues facing people back home, where I lived, in my community. On my part, I suppose I was on the lookout, however casually,

for an opportunity to serve locally. **It seemed like I had
been working on these issues everywhere but my own
backyard.**

It's hard to be a girl, or a woman, in poverty *anywhere*.
Too often we think about these people as existing somewhere else, in Africa, Asia, the Middle East. But they're here
as well, right where you live. Maybe not on your block or
street, but I promise you won't have to look very far.

> *Poverty and disease are not just things
> that happen somewhere else. They exist
> here, right in your own backyard—no
> matter who you are or where you live.*

As for me, when Robin texted, even though I was taken
aback at first, on a deeper level, it was what I always knew
was coming. I had been looking my whole life for that
opportunity to help and to be present and effective *where I
lived*—for my neighbors, my community. I had spent years
preparing for this moment, sharpening my skillset and
understanding of systems, policy, and human impact. This
meant that I was ready, when it counted, to be effective. It
meant that people like Robin knew I had the experience

and heart for this kind of work and that **I could now apply my abilities locally, through the vehicle of public service and elected positional leadership.**

If, on the other hand, my life had taken a different path, if I had gone to work selling cars or developed a reputation for being motivated just by salary, the opportunity would never have come. If I had worked outside my area of passion and not stayed true to my *why* and the issues I cared about, it would have never happened.

To be clear, if you want to sell cars, if that is your *why*, go after it with all your passion. But the point is, selling cars...that's someone *else's* why. Not mine. I cared about helping people in specific, critical ways. And I wanted to scale it up.

That didn't mean what came next would be easy for me.

MAKING YOURSELF UNCOMFORTABLE

Even though helping others was my zone of passion, it didn't mean it always came naturally. I still often had to put myself in situations that were unpleasant and even risky.

Sometimes I can be really lazy. My mom still calls me her "flop and read" girl. Trust me, **there are plenty of times**

when I'd rather just be comfy at home. Working with the Kiwanis, for example, sounds exciting and adventurous, and it was. But even when you're doing something wonderful and important like supporting volunteers running a prosthetic limb clinic in India, there's a part of you that just wants to be back with your family.

It's the same with my work as an elected official. When it's a cold winter day in the Midwest and I have to get up at the crack of dawn to go knock on doors...well, let's just say it takes a lot of effort to get out from under those warm bedcovers and hit the pavement. Coffee can be a miracle elixir some days!

In so many ways, I'm an unlikely politician. To be totally frank, I suffer from social anxiety. One of my best friends once told me I'm an introvert who is masquerading as an extrovert—and I believe that is true. When it came to my first campaign for state representative, I knew the only way I was going to have any chance of winning my race was to knock on thousands and thousands of doors. But it was so against my usual temperament and personality. I couldn't knock on a close friend's door, let alone a complete stranger's, without feeling anxious or embarrassed.

Too often, I second-guessed myself. Had my facts and opinions been vetted at the highest levels? Was the person whose door I was knocking on going to shred my arguments to bits?

Who was I to knock on these people's doors and ask for their vote?

It took me a while for this lesson to sink in, but what I eventually learned was: none of us are perfect. All we have is ourselves.

It took me months of knocking on doors to start to become more comfortable. At first, it felt almost like a walk of shame. But then there were those moments, when I was having a critical conversation with someone on a human level about what was most important to them, that made it all worth it. Their concerns were not always the same as mine. They'd have their own issues, but it was so valuable just to be able to listen to them. **It helped me learn what it meant to represent a diverse volume of people.**

But it took a great deal of internal discipline. The hot summer days were as bad as the winter ones. When it's over one hundred degrees out and you're sweating on someone's doorstep and your mascara melts into the creases around your eyes, let me tell you: it can be a very humbling experience. Some sweaty afternoons, people actually did a double-take when they looked at the professional campaign picture in the piece of literature I handed them and then looked back at my rumpled shirt and damp ponytail. It wasn't easy on the ego.

But I knew it wasn't about me. And it's the same for you. You have to let go of your ego and focus on engaging with the person in front of you. To ask for someone's vote, you have to connect with them. I knew I couldn't have these kinds of experiences and make these personal connections just by buying TV commercials and digital ads or by sending texts. **I had to actually visit with them, on their doorsteps, in their living rooms, at their kitchen tables.**

I hope that never changes. Serving your community is not just about tweeting or answering questions on a live online chat through a screen. It's about that back-and-forth, reciprocal, human conversation. It became so clear just how important that was, and as a shy person, I had to dig deep to find the gumption to do it.

It was so tiring. I didn't even dream most nights. I wore through three pairs of sneakers walking hundreds of miles on foot. There were too many early mornings and late nights to count. And then there was the sacrifice I had to put my family through. I wasn't there to take my turn making dinner, or cycle the laundry, or just hang out and be as present as I would like to with the ones I love. The clock was running and I needed every available moment dedicated to the project of getting elected.

Now, here I am, almost ten years later.

I've become a pretty good public speaker. I've grown a lot more comfortable with it over time and through practice. But even today, I question myself: *Did that make sense? Did I do a good enough job?* I second-guess my own performance and worry when I probably shouldn't and don't need to.

On the other hand, that's what keeps us humble, which is a good thing, I suppose. Maybe some of that questioning that goes on in our head is healthy, at least in moderation. It keeps us striving for excellence.

Let yourself be vulnerable. Take risks and **get comfortable with being uncomfortable** and inconvenienced.

Above all, put yourself out there so that, when your moment comes, you'll be in the right place at the right time. You may be the last person on the list to be called, but you have to be *on the list*.

And then when that opportunity does come, you have to be ready to say *yes*.

> *Let go of your ego and focus on your*
> issue *and the people you're helping.*

Beth White making her why clear to the public at the Indy Pride Parade.

BE READY TO
SAY YES

There's no way to know when a historic moment will open up in front of you. In fact, as I've seen time and again, often it happens when you least expect it. *Boom*, suddenly you're called upon to step up and be a decision-maker on the biggest of stages.

You can't know when lightning is going to strike—but you better be *ready* when that big opportunity comes around, or you'll miss out.

That means being true to yourself and following your *why* but also striving to always put yourself in roles of positional leadership so that you're in the right place and right time when the proverbial stars align.

Beth White was in such a position as County Clerk when her window of opportunity opened. In fact, she was the only County Clerk in the state of Indiana when a court decision gave same-sex couples the right to marry. (This was before the landmark 2015 civil rights case Obergefell v. Hodges, which legalized same-sex marriage across the whole country.) Immediately following the state ruling, Beth went into action and became the first elected official to marry same-sex couples in Indiana.

It was a remarkable distinction for her, an amazing achievement in an amazing career. But it didn't just come out of thin air. Beth had run for office as County Clerk because she'd always been passionate about running elections and running them properly. We've all learned in recent years just how important it is that every vote counts and every registered voter has access to the polls, whether we're living through a pandemic or natural disaster or just a common, everyday Tuesday.

Beth was driven by a burning desire to ensure everyone had a chance to make their voice heard as a citizen of this country. She was committed to making sure the election systems in her state were in place and properly run.

That was her *why*. And because she followed her *why* and put herself in an important role of positional leadership, she was ready to say *yes* when it counted.

Not all of Indiana was thrilled about the new law, of course. There was a great deal of controversy. But through it all, Beth led by example. I'll never forget the way she described rushing to the City Council building, opening the doors on that Valentine's Day and seeing the lines of eager couples waiting to be married.

How incredible Beth must have felt to play her part in such an important and historic occasion.

You can feel that too. It may still be far away. But if you're inspired and driven by whatever cause sets *your* hair on fire, if you have a servant-leader's heart and want to actually get things done, and if you follow your why and pursue positional leadership—then there's no reason why you can't be just like Beth.

When history calls, it will be *you*, not someone else, who has been handed the keys to the car.

Being ready when opportunity knocks takes preparation. It means sacrificing and operating outside of your comfort zone. But with practice, it becomes second nature.

When opportunity knocks, are you
going to be ready to say yes?

BEING READY POSITIONALLY

You may think you're ready in your heart and mind to be a leader. But are you ready positionally? Have you done the work, like Beth did?

You never want be caught out when the big opportunity arises, not ready for something you really desire. Instead, you want to feel confident that you've practiced and refined all the necessary skills, listened to the right people, and ensured that you can stand with confidence and respond to whatever challenge, ready to move forward.

There's nothing worse than getting that big break and then feeling like, *I want to say yes, but I know I'd be winging it*. Don't get caught unprepared. You may think your big opportunity is still years away. But it's not enough to have grand dreams about saving the world or saving crack babies from a hail of bullets. You need to be specific about your *why* and what you want to do. Then, you need to show up and actually do the work and build the relationships.

You also need to build up *yourself*: prepare your communications skills and your network so that when the time comes—and it will come—you're ready to say *yes*. Yes to running for office, starting your own organization, leading a movement for social reform.

You can't drive the car if you haven't studied the rules of the road and learned how to operate the vehicle.

DIVING INTO THE DEEP END

Preparing yourself to be ready to say *yes* often means having to get over your fears and insecurities. We all have them. In the previous chapter, I told you about my own social anxiety. Yes, it's scary and uncomfortable sometimes to talk to other human beings. Maybe especially so when you're young. But the good news is that it's something you can get over with practice. Volunteer to go door-to-door for candidates you believe in, and force yourself to talk to people about the issues that matter to them.

It's like going to the dentist. You dread it for days, you worry about what's going to happen, but then when you finally get there, the appointment is over in half an hour, no big deal—and you wind up feeling so much better for it.

This is true not just for public speaking but so many of the activities you're going to have to do to prepare yourself, the paces you're going to have to put yourself through. When it comes down to it, these things are really not that bad. But it's easy to get intimidated and create a kind of mental block.

Remember, it's just like with anything, any sport or learning a musical instrument: practice makes perfect. **Dive in with the very thing that most scares you, and just do it, again and again, until it loses its negative baggage.**

Keep at it and keep showing up.

Show up *where the people are*, at the community meetings where they are gathering to talk about crime in the neighborhood, or opening a dog park, or how to reduce litter on the street. Don't be shy, just pull up a chair, and join them. Get involved. Pick up some trash yourself. Connect with groups supporting your local humane society or pet shelter. There are any number of ways you can be a part.

Start out small and practice. Put yourself in ongoing contact with the people in your community. Let them inspire you and inform your approach to enacting cause-based positive change.

Ask questions and **learn how to really listen.**

THE SKILL OF LISTENING

Listening is a critical skill in just about any arena, but it's at the very core of becoming an effective advocate and change-maker. If you don't listen, you simply can't know all the facts, all the important details, the different facets and dimensions, of what's really going on in your community. You may think that you've got it all figured out already, but if you're not listening, you're not really present.

It's true that you can't walk in *everyone* else's shoes, but you can certainly learn from them—by asking the right questions and developing the art of listening.

It's all about being in the moment, focused on what the other person is saying to you, and genuinely trying to learn something new from them or be challenged in a different way. Doing this will sharpen your own motivation and also help you see your issue from a fresh perspective. You will very likely learn something about your cause that you had never considered before.

As I talked about in the previous chapter, knocking on doors helped me overcome my shyness—but it also helped me learn how to listen. Forcing myself to do these uncomfortable things, to put myself out there, go to community meetings, and more, is how I won my first race. But it is also what helped me pass my first bill as a legislator. In this case, the issue in question was not directly related to my *why* (fighting back against sexual assault), but it was important to my constituents.

Because I got out there and listened to people, I learned about a problem I never knew existed. In my neighborhood at the time, there were a lot of cash-for-gold stores, where you could take gold or silver jewelry and sell it for cash on the spot. Then, the item would be melted down immediately for commodity value, so obviously after you sold it you couldn't recover it. Why is that a problem? Well, anybody could walk in with somebody else's jewelry and sell it then and there. Where I lived, there were a lot of residential break-ins. Robbers knew it was easy to get their hands on people's stuff. I was a victim of a robbery myself at one point. But I didn't realize the particulars of this problem until I started talking to people in the neighborhood. It was a big deal to *them* and to a lot of people where I lived.

It wasn't only jewelry that got stolen. But, as I soon learned, if your electronics were stolen, often the item would show up at a pawn store. Pawn stores have a stricter policy. They hold the item for twelve days, take a photo of it, and publish it in an online catalog. They also take down the name and ID of the person selling it to them. So, of course, it discourages thieves.

But there was nothing like that with the cash-for-gold stores. The police would always say the same thing: "You may recover your TV that was stolen, but you'll never get Grandma's wedding ring back."

At the time, I remember I was happy to listen to people and learn about this specific, on-the-ground problem they were experiencing. I knew I cared about criminal justice, about keeping people safe. And **here was a problem that I would have continued to be completely ignorant of if I hadn't knocked on all those doors.**

Knocking on all those doors, I started to see patterns and trends. The more people you talk to, the more you realize, *Oh, this isn't an anomaly. This is an issue that lots of people have in common.* And they were concerns that you didn't necessarily hear about on the news or from other sources. You had to hear about them directly from the people.

GETTING INTO FIGHTING SHAPE

That was the genesis of the first bill I ever got passed. I was able get a new law through the system that regulated gold-for-cash stores and helped reduce crime in this particular category. None of it would have been possible if I hadn't knocked on all those doors, gone to those community meetings, and *showed up*.

Doing so introduced me to an issue that I knew nothing about. Crucially, it also got me into fighting shape so that I was ready and fired up to take on the problem and to do whatever it took to fix it.

Even though it was perhaps a small victory, I look back on it with pride. It was my first time in the ring, and I felt like Rocky.

There would be many more battles to fight and many more triumphs. But maybe even more important to my growth and development were the later legislative disappointments and races I lost.

Always listen, always learn—whether people can vote for you or not.
Win or lose, how you deal with success, loss, and yourself truly matters.

8

LIKE TEFLON

Before becoming president—and going into the history books as one of the greatest American leaders of all time, during probably the most dire crisis our country has ever faced, the Civil War—Abraham Lincoln experienced a number of losses and setbacks, both political and personal.

He was only twenty-three when he ran for his first office, state legislature, and lost. But it taught him patience and resilience.

By this point in his life, Lincoln had already gone through quite a bit of struggle. He wasn't someone who came from elite circles or from the Ivy League. He grew up poor, moved around a lot, and had to support his family. He put himself through school. Tragically, he lost his mother when he was only nine.

An outsider in so many ways, his dream to run for state legislature was driven by a desire to represent the common man—folks who had come from similar backgrounds and lived through the kinds of experiences he had.

But it wasn't to be. Not at first. He tried, and he lost.

Two years later, at age twenty-five, he tried again, and this time he won. It was the start of a career in government, crafting law and trying to make the world a better place. But it wasn't all smooth sailing. He suffered a number of subsequent losses as well. In 1838, he ran for Speaker of the House—and failed.

Then, in 1843, still a young man, he ran for Congress but did not receive the party's nomination. He lost the opportunity to move his candidacy forward but learned from that failed campaign how to be a better politician. In 1846, he ran again. This time, not only did he win his party's nomination but also a seat in the US Congress. He went to Washington, DC, to serve his country.

But he felt called toward something even bigger and more significant. In 1854, he ran for US Senate. He lost. In

1858, he ran and lost yet again.

Meanwhile, through these years, he suffered a number of setbacks in his personal life. He went bankrupt. He had a nervous breakdown. But **it all informed the man he was to become, who would lead us through the war that almost destroyed us as a country.** And it was because of his history—of not just winning but also losing—that Lincoln was able to become that great leader. Through all the failures and setbacks, he learned to listen to others, and to step up with courage to any challenge, knowing that he might not achieve his goal, but he would never stop trying.

Lincoln's losses informed his eventual presidency and critical leadership just as much as his successes did—in fact, probably more so.

He led with empathy and wisdom. He made us acknowledge that *all* of our people are citizens with rights and that no human being should be enslaved by another.

If he had won every race, or if had lived a gilded life of privilege divorced from the reality of how most Americans really lived and thought, Lincoln likely wouldn't have become the same man, a person of such heart and integrity.

In fact, it was during a Senate race that he *lost* where he initially came to fame. Debating his opponent, Stephen A. Douglas, he talked for the first time in a big way about the evil and injustice of slavery. These Lincoln-Douglas debates were where he truly stepped into his own and earned his battle scars. He may have lost the race for Senate from Illinois. But the experience made him scale up his game and aspire to even higher office.

These debates gave him the opportunity to show positional leadership and speak with moral courage to the American people. The experience set himself on a path to eventually save our country from tremendous shame and loss and allow us to re-boot, in a sense, and in a way that was much more consistent with the values of our founders and our citizenry. (Of course, the battle for civil rights was only just beginning.)

Sometimes even when you lose, like Lincoln did against Douglas, people take notice of how you carry yourself—and it can lead to all kinds of other opportunities.

I have always found it compelling, too, that Lincoln didn't wait to serve and fight for what he believed in. He sought a life of leadership and jumped in the game at an early age.

Throughout your own life, you are going to win some and lose some, as the saying goes. But **the best leaders, like Lincoln, are able to mine those bumps in the road for all the insight and resilience they bring.**

You are going to have tough battles ahead. But if you face them with strength and courage, even if you lose along the way—*especially* if you lose—you will come out Teflon on the other side.

Unstoppable.

WINNING IS GREAT, BUT LOSING IS NOT THAT BAD

Often, it's the journey that matters most, as much as the results. Yes, we all want to attain our goal and make a change in the world. But we are leaving money on the table when we don't mine the experience of *losing* for all the benefits that come with trying.

Now, of course, I don't mean to imply you will wake up the morning after your loss feeling like Teflon. It's a process. You have to be intentional and spend some time in your own head thinking through how you've changed and grown and doing a self-inventory of the strengths and weaknesses you showed. How are you going to take this experience and apply it to your next opportunity?

The loss will still sting. But you can't dwell on it. Your focus needs to be on how much better prepared you are now for the next opportunity. You're never going to be perfect. There is no perfect. When I say "like Teflon," it's more about your grit. You're always going to have feelings. But through losses, you'll have learned the hard way what's at stake. You'll see firsthand how the laws that you had hoped to pass, and all the goals you had set, are now sadly going unaccomplished. **You'll realize your voice and effort are still crucially needed, probably even more so than before.**

Not only will you have stepped up your game in so many ways, but your resolve will also be that much stronger. You'll be closer than before to identifying what your uniquely powerful role can be in your community, and across the broader world. You'll have a better understanding of your *why* and how you approach doing good for others.

You'll be stronger because now you've seen it. Done it. You've been there. You know how bad things can get, but you also know how badly you're needed—and how much better the world can be with all the hard work and elbow grease of you and others like you who care. You have a better understanding of the positive impact you can make.

And when you get there, you know you'll have done it the right way, with honor and integrity—and a servant-leader's heart.

As a direct result of your efforts, and especially all your prior losses and setbacks, you'll invite new opportunities that you could have never imagined before.

LOSING MY RACE

Standing in front of 1,000 people to give a concession speech is traumatic, especially when almost every person in that room really expected you to win. You feel so deeply how you've disappointed them, failed not only yourself but also those around you.

Then **you wake up the next morning to that hard reality. You didn't make it.** It's over, done. I was warned that the most difficult part of losing is the quiet. The phone stops ringing. People don't know what to say. It's almost as if someone died. They avoid you because they don't have the words for the difficult conversation required or to share their condolences with you.

I had been warned, and that's what I was expecting. But that's not what happened.

The morning after I lost the race for Lieutenant Governor of Indiana, I woke up to hundreds of texts and countless missed calls. In fact, it didn't stop all day. One of the first people to reach out was my friend, Rabbi Sandy Sasso. In particular, she told me how upset she and her friends were over the results of the presidential election. They wanted to talk about it and hear what I thought. Even though I had lost my race too, they still wanted me to come meet with them and kind of *reframe* some of the losses, as well as the pain they were feeling, so that they could be more productive and forward-thinking.

Of course, I said yes. We set a date, but then before the day arrived, Sandy called again and said, "You know what? I know I told you it was going to be just ten women, but it's actually looking like it will be more than that. So, I booked a private room at a restaurant. Are you still willing to come speak?"

"Of course I am," I responded.

But then Sandy called back the next day and said, "You know what, Christina? I think we're going to have closer to one hundred women. We are moving the event to my friend Jenny Nelson William's funeral home up in the next town over because it's got a big gathering room and we can fit more people in there. So many folks who want to have this conversation about what's next."

"Well, great!" I said. "I'll be there. I can't wait."

The morning of the event, she called me once again! "You'd better get there early, Christina, because we might have 200 people and parking is going to get scarce. I don't want you to have to worry about finding a parking spot when you're coming to speak."

I did what she said. Got there early. I couldn't believe what happened next: 500 people came out. They were crammed in corners, overflowing into the hallways and even outside in the parking lot on a cold November night. Not only that, but 500 *more* people had to be turned away. The BBC showed up with their cameras. There were other women who had been invited to speak alongside me, including my mentors Betty Cockram and Sheila Seuss Kennedy, and they were all wonderful. It was such a special moment, where people really came together and set politics aside.

We had Republicans, Democrats, Independents, and people who hadn't even voted. Everyone just wanted to share, and listen, and think about what was next for our community.

My loss, and the amazing response at Sandy's event and others, showed me that my work wasn't over. Importantly, it gave me the opportunity to encourage others to be part of the solution too. First thing for them was to get out and vote. Don't just sit around and watch debates and talk about it and have your opinions. Do something about it.

Losing the race for Lieutenant Governor was one of the best things that had ever happened to me.

Losing the race also gave me a voice I wouldn't have had otherwise. I had already been a passionate and effective advocate, but because of the way those dice landed, I was able to move in some exciting new directions in my career.

Because of the way I showed up during that race, people now looked to me as an expert and public voice on the issues I cared about, particularly preventing sexual assault. **Before I lost the election, I wasn't a pundit on broadcast television. I wasn't writing a column for a leading business publication.** I was just somebody's neighbor or someone you'd run into at the grocery store. But now, people had seen—and I think vetted—my opinions because I had put them out there formally as a candidate and had debated, listened, refined, and researched my thinking and approach to doing good for people.

Despite my loss, people now turn to me as a voice of leadership.

When we try and fail—and come out Teflon—we emerge poised to apply that experience to the next thing.

I couldn't help my friend after her assault when we were teens, but I was determined to follow up somehow, so I learned the rules, and now I changed the law. She doesn't know it, but she inspired my career and gave me the strength to fight.

KNOW THE RULES

When I was a candidate running for office and knocking on people's doors—talking to them about what I thought was important and listening to them about what *they* needed—I quickly learned there were many issues that weren't even remotely on my radar. I realized I didn't always know when people in my community might be in difficult, or in dangerous, situations that were totally foreign to me.

I'd be knocking on doors in these suburban neighborhoods that felt extremely safe: the kind where everyone mows their lawn and plants pretty flowers. But **what I** didn't realize was that people felt unsafe, and for a reason I had never imagined.

I walked up to one home that had a cute yard and a sign that said, "If you want to buy local honey, leave your name and address, and we'll follow up with you." How cool. They were selling homemade honey. I had always made a point of trying to support local businesses, and this was a community I hoped to represent. So, I left my name and number and walked on to the next house.

There, sitting in the driveway on a couple of folding chairs, were a man and woman. I walked up and began to introduce myself but was quickly interrupted. "Do you know what this is?" the man said, waving a manila envelope in my face. He seemed kind of angry and upset.

"No, I don't" I responded.

"Well, I'm going to tell you. There are 327 bee carcasses in here."

"Wow!"

"And this is just what I swept up *this afternoon*," he continued. "Come with me."

I followed him through his house, to his back door, and stepped up on his deck. There, he pointed over the fence to his neighbor's yard. It was swarming with bees. I counted at least twelve beehives, but all around it was just a thick dark fog: millions of bees buzzing around like crazy.

Then, the man pointed over to his pool. "I can't even use it anymore. I just skimmed that out this morning!" The surface of his pool was indeed covered in bees.

"What breaks my heart about all of this," he continued, "is that my granddaughter can no longer come over to my home. She's allergic. There are many people in this neighborhood who are deathly allergic to bees. It's not an uncommon allergy anymore. And now we have these people living right next door who are producing honey commercially."

Whereas my first impression to the neighbors' sign had been, "Oh, what a great thing, I can buy local honey," now I was seeing a totally different side to the story.

For the people who lived next door, it was a nightmare.

IF YOU DON'T KNOW THE ANSWERS, YOU CAN AT LEAST KNOW WHERE TO FIND THEM

I didn't choose to run for office because I was trying to save people from bee stings, of course. Or even from a life-threatening bee allergy. But I *was* running to provide for their public safety. And here—in this nice neighborhood, in a district I was hoping to represent—was something that I hadn't even imagined could be a problem.

You're going to encounter a lot of mysterious issues like this. Some of them might relate to the causes you really care about, like making sure people feel safe in their homes. But then what do you do? Who do you turn to for something so unusual, so specific?

> *What's the protocol when someone has twelve beehives and is producing honey in their backyard? Whose job is it to even police that?*

As it turned out, regulating amateur beekeeping was nobody's job. I learned the hard way that there really weren't any state laws about this. The people who lived on that block didn't know the rules, and I didn't know the rules either. But I wanted to represent them and help them out. I also wanted to help the business owners. I wanted to find a solution that worked for all. But first, I had to educate myself.

The rules aren't always going to be obvious. It helps to be someone who knows where to look. In my case, even though I didn't have any familiarity with this particular situation, or the laws that might govern it, I knew how government worked. I knew there were a few different options we could pursue.

I worked with the city counselor to get the zoning changed. We came up with a solution that would support the rights of the business owners to produce honey in a safe way and support the rights of the neighbors to enjoy peace and safety on their property. Best of all, their granddaughter was once again able to come over and cool off on a hot summer's day in their pool.

KNOW HOW TO WORK THE SYSTEM

Learn civics. Know the rules and how they work. You can even learn how to *change* a rule by petitioning the city council. You can also lobby to create a new rule that becomes law and provides for public safety for years, even generations, to come.

Study how a bill becomes law and how you can step up and get something done. Knowing the rules, understanding how government works, can enable you to affect change on behalf of people, like the neighbors with the pool, who don't have the knowledge or resources to do it for themselves.

In most cases, the rules already exist, and there's advantage in them. If you know how government operates, you're already one up in terms of being positioned to advance your agenda for good. You know, for example, that you **don't talk to your state representatives about curbs and sewers. You go to your city counselor, or your county commissioner.**

Sadly, in most high schools today, we don't spend enough time studying the rules of government and how things work. We may learn about American history but not about civics more broadly. We learn how our government came to be, hundreds of years ago, but not how it actually works, or is meant to work, in the present day!

Imagine if our education system taught us how to actually use government, particularly local government and its different levers, to make change happen in our communities. That's the most important thing, and it's what we're missing.

Rule the rules so they don't rule you.

You can influence the issues you care about where you live, even if you're under eighteen. You might not be able to vote yet, but you can still be appointed to serve on boards and commissions in your communities. You can participate in these platforms that hold real influence over decisions that you're going to have to live with for years to come.

YOU HAVE MORE LEVERAGE THAN YOU THINK

Maybe you live in a neighborhood where they want to co-op the public park to build a block of apartments and call it a "development." What can you do about it? Well, you might just be able to serve on the neighborhood committee that gets to vote on whether it supports the development or not, *before* the vote goes to your city council. You might be able to have a say right now.

Look into it. Call your mayor's office. Speak to the person who appoints boards and commissions. Show up at your neighborhood association meetings. Ask around. Find out what the rules are where you live. They are different all over the country, from state to state, sometimes from city to city, town to town. **Know the rules where you are.** Make it your job to find out. That information is usually only a phone call or Google search away.

Knowing how the rules work enables you to influence decisions throughout the process. Know when the deadlines are for bills to be heard in committee. Know when the Governor needs to sign your bill. Know when everything has to be drafted and filed. Know when you have to convince the chairman of the committee to hear a bill in order for it to move forward that year.

These things are important because, **if you're determined and dogged and know the rules, you can be in the right place at the right time to ensure the right thing happens to keep your cause alive.**

> *Knowing the rules better than your*
> *opposition can give you a leg up.*

Not everyone can be present when laws are being made, but they can observe and listen. In most states, you can watch your city government and city council meet. It's available online. You can watch your general assembly. You can watch C-Span and debate from the floor in the US Congress.

You can stay on top of deadlines and pivotal actions, whether your issue is stuck in court, or stuck in Congress. Even if you're not physically there, you can still be there, at the right place and the right time. A phone call, a letter to the editor, a visit to your legislator—these go a long way to making sure your bill is eligible for that vote when it needs to be, before it's too late.

THE POWER OF LOCAL GOVERNMENT

When it comes to politics, local government is not the sexiest thing in the world, I know. But it is *important*. Local government influences your life where you are, in an untold number of ways, many of which would surprise you. Think about the bees. Much of that came down to local government.

Local government is what determines how clean your streets are. Is your local government going to sell parkland out from under you? Do they have a recycling program? How do they treat neglected animals, or the elderly, or young children? Much of that is the domain of local government, and there is an opportunity for you to serve in it, sometimes before you even turn eighteen.

Local government is a great place to incubate and learn the rules *where you are*—to get a better idea of how to specifically address solutions as part of your bigger cause.

So don't wait. This is something you can do *now*. Yes, it's different in every community and municipality. That's why you need to take on a modest research project: find out for yourself what the situation is in your neck of the woods. Call City Hall. Ask around in your neighborhood. Show up to local meetings. Look at who's serving on the boards. Ask lots of questions.

Sure, you'll run into the occasional jerk, but most people are going to want to help you. And more often than not, they don't really care about your politics. They see a young person inquiring about, and taking interest in, his or her home community. That's what matters. And that's what will make them want to help you.

A GAME OF CHESS

Knowing the rules is kind of like a game of chess. You might want to defeat your opponent and have strong opinions about winning, but just cheering on the sidelines isn't going to do you a whole lot of good. You have to know how to play the game and play it well—at least as well as your opponent.

It's something you have control over—even at your age now. You can know the rules. It might take a little work, some study, and a lot of conversations. But there is power in those rules. It's the power that puts you in the right place at the right time when critical decisions are made.

Making laws is like watching sausage get made. That's true in some respects. It can be ugly when you see all that goes into making that sausage. So ugly, in fact, that you might not want to eat at all, now that you know what's inside.

But at the end of the day, it's really important that *you* know what went into that sausage. There are people who don't want to know, and that's fine. But it's not okay for you.

To be an effective change-maker, you have to know the rules.

Know what goes into the sausage!

Why not you? Indiana Supreme Court Chief Justice Loretta Rush gave me the oath of office. I hope to see you take that oath someday. We need you.

BUILD YOUR CHARACTER, NOT YOUR RÉSUMÉ

There's a great deal of research out there showing that young people are feeling depressed and lesser-than as they scroll the never-ending streams of their friends' social media. In fact, there has been a clear spike in teen suicide that is arguably linked to this phenomenon.

What are we to make of this alarming state of affairs?

We all know that people come across differently online: with their perfectly filtered photos and perfectly curated presentation, they make it seem—even if this is not their conscious intention—like their lives are always firing on all cylinders, and that all is going according to plan.

It is in this context that authenticity becomes so import-ant. People are hungry for the reality, the raw, unvarnished truth. Deep down, we all know there is no such thing in life as *perfect*.

> *Living with authenticity is more*
> *important today than ever.*

You are never going to be perfect as a change-maker. (Promise: I am certainly far from perfect.) Yes, you *are* going to be incredibly good at it and accomplished, but not perfect.

So, be honest and open in how you present yourself. Don't hide your imperfections—show who you really are. **Own your life in all its texture.** Maybe you don't have the fancy degrees that others do. Maybe you feel like you're not cool enough or good-looking enough. It's okay. We all have those insecurities. You will stand out all the more when you let go of those anxieties and show who you really are.

Follow the words of Lewis Carroll and be "what you would seem to be."

It means speaking with your own voice. It means being transparent and expressing yourself honestly.

Don't fall into the trap of
becoming a people-pleaser.

Often, when people first step into the public eye, they make the mistake of always trying to please. It's understandable: you're putting yourself out there for the first time, in front of folks you don't know and have never met. Then, they're writing back and making comments about you. There's a temptation to respond in a way that will make you look good in their eyes. But **what's *most* important is not how you look but rather communicating in a way that's true to you, your identity, school of thought, and everything you're trying to achieve.**

Say you're talking about the issue of school shootings. You may well find yourself in some really difficult conversations, confronted by people who disagree with you, who don't like you, who come from very different backgrounds than you. That's okay. Don't let it bend who you are and what you believe in. You still need to be you.

LETTING GO OF THE
RÉSUMÉ-OBSESSED MENTALITY

Not only is it important to resist the airbrushed version of reality on social media, but also the whole idea of *perfect* in your own life—especially when it comes to getting perfect grades, having the perfect résumé, and so on.

We live in a culture of grade-grubbing and résumé-stuffing. It's become so academically competitive that we've lost sight of what really matters.

Obviously, if you want to step into positional power, you do have to participate in these endeavors. It's the only way to get ahead. On the other hand, if you're not careful, you can develop a kind of tunnel-vision that distracts you from your true end-goals.

Academics are important, but always
keep your eyes on the (bigger) prize.

We all know it's more difficult than ever to get into college. There are more applications, more requirements, more *everything*. It wasn't so long ago that institutions of higher education didn't really care so much about your extracurricular activities or how you expressed yourself in your application essay. They just wanted your test scores and your grades.

It's a different world now. Which, of course, is good in many, many ways. After all, students are more than just their grades and standardized test scores! But the new landscape also creates new pressures. I encourage you to keep a level head about it all. So much is outside of your control anyway. Do the best job you can. Do a thorough self-inventory. Think about who you are, what you've done, and how you can best present yourself. But don't drive yourself crazy.

There's never just that one opportunity, one school, one scholarship. There are many pathways to your future. When one is closed off, others lie in the wings. You just have to be on the lookout for them. In fact, there may be a *better* opportunity directly behind this one, something you never even imagined for yourself.

You are part of a generation where you're going to live many lives and have many iterations of yourself. You're not going to work at the same place for fifty years like your grandparents did. You're living in a time of accelerated change, driven by technology. This means you're going to have to be more nimble, flexible, and open to other opportunities than young people were in the past.

There is so much that is going to change during your lifetime, and so much of it is still a mystery. But what *is* a guarantee is that **people are going to need change-makers like you, who are inspired to do good things.** That's never going to go away.

WE'RE NEVER GOING TO LIVE IN A PERFECT WORLD

We're *always* going to need champions like you who are prepared to step up—and your preparation for this future goes beyond building your résumé, getting this or that credential, graduating from law school or medical school, or learning a certain kind of software.

Part of your preparation, in fact maybe the biggest part, is going to involve how you navigate the uncertain times you live through. What insights and motivation will you draw from these experiences toward doing better for the people who come after you?

Focus on exploration, on understanding who you really are, and building your character.

Life is about a lot more than passing the next test, getting the right grade, etc.

There are probably a lot of people around you who *think* they know what's best for you: parents, siblings, teachers. And for the most part, they probably *do* have your best interests at heart. They want you to be happy, healthy, and self-sufficient. They want you to accomplish good things in life. But **there are aspects of you that they can't possibly know or fully understand because they're not you.** The only person who gets to be you is you. You know yourself like now one else, and only you can decide what *your* best path forward may be.

To be clear, your parents and teachers love you, they think well of you, and they recognize your skill and intellect, all the talent you have. They also believe they know best how to apply it in a way that will help you find that sweet spot, that intersection of your talent and ability with potential career opportunities.

But it's about more than just career per se: do they know as well as you do what the particular, positionally powerful change-maker role might be that is not only important and impactful but authentic and meaningful to you? By all means listen to them. Keep an open mind and get advice from them and everyone. But there's only one person who can make the final decision about your future, and that's you.

Don't get me wrong: these are complicated matters. It's definitely a balance. In some cases, you may be getting advice that you *don't* want to hear, but the truth is you *need* to hear it. Other times, however, you will need to trust in yourself. **One of the hardest parts of being a young person is knowing when to take the advice of elders and when to take a pass.**

Sometimes there are even people around you who may sabotage you. Always keep your eyes open. It's easy for folks to give advice when they're not the ones who will be responsible for the consequences. If you're not careful, you'll be not only taking on someone's advice but taking on a boatload of personal debt!

The person giving you advice isn't necessarily the one paying for you to go to law school, for example. You are. And that's expensive (to put it mildly). Be cautious and thoughtful as you consider what it is that will set you up for that next thing.

> *Your path may be different than most of your friends, and that's okay. It may be completely different than what your family has always imagined for you—and that's okay too.*

THE FULL CIRCLE

When I got pregnant at age nineteen, a single mom, I gave birth to a boy I named Owen. Even as a very little kid, he had a great sense of humor. He was smart and articulate. I always thought he'd be perfect in the courtroom. My vision for him was that one day he'd be a courtroom attorney, an Atticus Finch in the courtroom, protecting the innocent.

As it turns out, now that he's a grown man, Owen is finding his success and happiness in a completely different arena, on stage as a stand-up comedian. Do I wish he had pursued more traditional employment where he would get regular health insurance and a 401(k) plan? Part of me does. But then I see him doing what he loves, on the road, at gigs, bringing humor and insights into people's lives—and I couldn't be prouder.

At the end of the day, who am I to make the decision for him? He's finding success and meaning for himself. I'm actually glad he didn't listen to me. He stepped off the cliff into uncertainty to pursue his *why*—and is doing it his way.

Follow your own heart. Dream big.

Now that you've got some skin in the game and have been working on yourself—trying to understand your *why*—you are well positioned to *jump* into your role of positional leader and change-maker.

You have cast your sights well beyond narrow academic achievement toward change-making on a much bigger scale.

Keep your eyes open for your big moment. You're needed, and that moment could come at any time.

WHAT COMES NEXT

So, having come to the end of the book, now it's your turn...
where do you want to take this?

When Abraham Lincoln was twenty-three years old and
lost his first race for state representative, he probably didn't
have the audacity to dream that he might one day become
President of the United States of America. Or maybe he did.
Who knows what he was thinking about when he was your
age? What were his fears? How did he prepare and visualize
to be able to say *yes* when his moment arrived? How was he
inspired to take action and move forward?

You probably don't think about yourself as the next Abe
Lincoln. But maybe you should.

Our era will have its very own heroes and champions. Lincoln probably didn't anticipate he would be leading the country during a time of civil war. It just goes to show: none of us know what's coming next.

But we do know that **if we prepare, if we work on our character, our skillset—if we develop an understanding of the issues we care about and put ourselves out there— we can be ready when the opportunity presents itself.**

Our era will have its own Abe Lincolns.

What about you? Who do you want to be?

Do you have a good heart? Do you have a good mind? Are you in it for the right reasons?

Again, I think you already know the answers. Or you wouldn't be reading this book.

So, before I sign off, let me ask you one more question: **why not you?**

ACKNOWLEDGMENTS

Those days when your heart and your head demand that you curl up and hide under the covers (or run away and hide) are real.

But you know what? If you have come this far with me, reader, then you need to know this truth as well. It is very possible that someone you have grown to count on drops out of your life because of your convictions or your campaign. And it will sting, maybe for a very long time.

That said, you will also meet the most wonderful people in life—people you can't even begin to imagine in this moment. At this moment, they are strangers to you, yet they are people who will rally around and carry you through those days you long to lock yourself away. People who will knock on doors in the worst summer heat, people who will make calls for you and even donate money to you, to your *why*, when it is money they could really use for something else.

Please understand that I truly have too many people to thank in these limited pages. Writing these acknowledgments was the most difficult and emotional part of writing this book. It is nothing short of overwhelming. For this reason, my heart is full of names, faces, moments, and deep gratitude.

Credit for this book, however, must be shared with my dear friends Kip and Robin Tew. Thank you for your friendship and that fatal text offering soup, football, and a truly wild ride. I wouldn't have had the chance to learn these lessons without you.

John Gregg, you truly are a workhorse and not a show pony. Thank you for showing me how to keep a dream alive and living the values of hard work and humor.

Mark Chait, thank you for guiding me through a difficult writing process and finding order and meaning in it all, and to Erin Mellor, for getting this into print, finally. Natalie Aboudaoud, I truly appreciate your professionalism and publishing acumen.

Yet, of course, it all starts at home—my first home, created by my parents, Margot and Steven Hale, and my brothers Mike and Steve. I love you deeply, and the resilience you have all cultivated in me has been indispensable in life.

Philip Goddard, Big Bunny, the lessons of friendship and loyalty that you continue to share with me were not expected but something I have learned to count on every day. Everyone needs a Big Bunny in their life, and it is one of my greatest pleasures to witness the joy you earned the hard way.

Phil Garrett, thank you for being such a good man and rising to incredible challenges your entire life.

Terry and Cinda Monday, how I count on and appreciate your time and warm welcomes, even when just off of the trail.

Owen, with you in mind, I can always see the right path forward. Channeling your inner sense of justice always makes it easier for me to do the hard thing.

To my husband Chris, I love you deeply. Win or lose, you always have my back. Can't wait to figure out what our next venture will be together...maybe I could talk you into letting me manage your first campaign?

And finally, of course, dogs. Dog love is real, and running for office is a very intense (if worthwhile) experience.

Pippin, Grace, and Pinecone even appreciated the smell of my sneakers after a long day knocking on doors. Win or lose, they are loyal and true. And what a wonderful thing that is.

ABOUT THE AUTHOR

The best way to describe Christina Hale is as an average person driven to—and successful in—making an exceptional difference. She worked her way through college as a proud single mother and served as a nonprofit executive for Kiwanis International, fulfilling a variety of roles that included chief communications officer and executive director for Kiwanis Youth Programs worldwide. A former state legislator for the Indiana General Assembly and the first Latina to run for statewide office in Indiana, Christina earned a reputation for bipartisanship and resolve. In 2021, Christina was appointed by the Biden-Harris Administration to head communications for the U.S. International Development Finance Corporation. She continues to fight against sexual violence and advocate for youth and democracy.

CPSIA information can be obtained
at www.ICGtesting.com
Printed in the USA
BVHW041243280722
643233BV00017B/716/J